Secrets of

DIVINATION

Secrets of
DIVINATION

JOHN ASTROP

DK Publishing, Inc.

LONDON, NEW YORK, SYDNEY, DELHI, PARIS, MUNICH, and JOHANNESBURG

This book was conceived, designed, and produced by
THE IVY PRESS LIMITED,
The Old Candlemakers, Lewes, East Sussex BN7 2NZ

Art director *Peter Bridgewater*
Publisher *Sophie Collins*
Designers *Kevin Knight, Jane Lanaway*
Project editor *Caroline Earle*
Picture researcher *Vanessa Fletcher and Trudi Valter*
Photography *Guy Ryecart*
Illustrations *Richard Lloyd, Andrew Kulman,*
Stephen Raw, Sarah Young
Three-dimensional models *Mark Jamieson*

First published in The United States of America in 2001 by
DK PUBLISHING, INC.
95 Madison Avenue, New York, New York 10016

Copyright © 2001 The Ivy Press Limited

A Cataloging-in-Publication record is
available from the Library of Congress

ISBN 0-7894-7777-7

Originated and printed by
Hong Kong Graphics and Printing Ltd., China

see our complete
catalog at
www.dk.com

CONTENTS

Tarot
Tarot cards are one of the most popular methods of divination. Nowadays there are all sorts of tarot decks to choose from.

HOW TO USE THIS BOOK *Secrets of Divination* is an introduction to a multitude of divinatory systems, including tarot, astrology, dowsing, runes, geomancy, and numerology. Each section begins with a history of each divinatory method; this is followed by practical instructions on how each method works, combined with detailed explanations about the subject in question. Even though these methods have their origins in ancient times, they can all be applied successfully today. You can experiment with these methods, to help you when faced with difficult decisions, or you can use them simply for fun.

Learning Divination

The aim of this book is to encourage the reader to experiment and enjoy learning how to develop their divinatory skills. Divination today combines modern methods with ancient wisdom, and this book enables the reader to use this knowledge to gain fascinating insights into their own and other people's past, present, and future.

Basic information
Beautifully illustrated color spreads give you the basic information you need to know about each subject.

Handling the cards

THE MINOR ARCANA

The minor arcana is much like an ordinary playing-card deck and comprises 56 cards divided into four suits, which in most decks are Swords, Wands, Cups, and Coins or Pentacles. Each suit has ten cards numbered 1 to 10, and four court cards usually called king, queen, knight, and page. The numbers 1 to 10 generally refer to events in the reading and the court cards to people on the life of the questioner, in earlier decks, the numbered cards were illustrated only with the appropriate number of Swords, Cups, Wands, etc. There are many other decks today where the minor arcana is completely illustrated, showing a more detailed picture of the card's meaning.

Love
Love and relationships are always described by the Cup suit. This corresponds to the expression of ideas related to emotions and feelings.

Wands
Events to do with work and creativity.

Swords
Events to do with ideas and communication.

Cups
Events to do with love, pleasure, sensitivity, and fertility.

Communication
Those with the gift of good communication, the ability to speak coherently, and express ideas fluently are shown in the court cards of the suit of Swords.

Pentacles (coins)
Events to do with finance, economics, and stability.

Practical advice
Full-color spreads explain how each method works and show the divinatory tools that are used for each one.

Some Famous Birth Charts

Here follow four famous birth charts—the position of the planets at the time of birth indicates the characteristics that led them to succeed in their chosen fields.

Margaret Thatcher
Britain's first female prime minister, known as the "Iron Lady," has magnetic Scorpio on her ascendant, while Saturn in Scorpio rising shows the almost ruthless determination to make her mark in life. The diplomatic Libran Sun has acquired a hard edge and here we see another Moon in Leo indicating the need to be in the public eye. However, Venus in Sagittarius in the first house shows that she has the ability to smile sweetly and get her own way when the arguments become intense.

Iron Lady
Scorpio, her ascendant sign, is ruled by Mars. The corresponding metals of Mars are iron and steel, aptly explaining her iron will.

Venus Williams
The winner of the ladies' championship at Wimbledon in 2000 has Sun Gemini, Moon Leo, and Mercury setting her in the public eye. Pluto in the first house on her Libran ascendant indicates her drive to succeed. Venus is close to the Sun in her chart, which shows her easy manner in interviews.

Superman
It is typical of Pisce clients consuming the ascendant, as in Christopher Reeve's chart that this is a life of revolutionary destiny.

Christopher Reeve
A superman with a superman's chart, Reeve was a perfect movie for the comic-strip hero. When disaster suddenly struck in real life in the form of paralysis after a fall from a horse, his own heroism took over. Pluto in Leo on the ascendant, and trine Mars in the fifth house, indicate enormous power and bravery, and signify the archetypal reckless-hero type. Jupiter in the tenth house is square Pluto. This promises that he will never leave the public eye or be forgotten by his admirers, despite the transformation in his life.

Steven Spielberg
The brilliant filmmaker and storyteller has an adventurous Sagittarian Sun in the sixth house, making him far seeking, but perfectionist, in his work. Opposite the Sun is the revolutionary, sometimes eccentric Uranus, which adds the theme of sudden, sharp shocks to his movies. The Moon, Jupiter, and Venus in Scorpio in the fifth house indicate creative passion and intensity and emphasis on human ties with an extraterrestrial aspect.

Storyteller
(With Pisces on the midheaven (career), the ability to visualize and fantasize would have been an incredible asset to the imaginative nature of Steven Spielberg.)

Analysis
Black-and-white spreads give more information on each divinatory method.

CASTING METHODS

Yarrow sticks
The traditional yarrow sticks, which are hard to find, can be replaced with ceramic satay skewers from your local supermarket (or remove the pointed ends.

The standard texts of the I Ching are lengthy and quite obscure on first reading. Although the ideal of the various "commentaries" is complex, with much symbolism, the principle is very simple. The traditional way of producing a reading is equally time consuming, but there are several alternatives you can use that take only minutes to produce a good result.

Coins and cards
It is now possible to find replicas of traditional Chinese coins, which can be used in your own throws. There are also several I Ching card decks that can be used. Casting methods.

Doing a reading
The simplest way is when to do a reading is to use three ordinary coins. There is another, more elaborate, method that uses 50 "yarrow" sticks. Although this is conducive to a gently contemplative approach to a reading, it requires much practice and a bare essential when one has gained more knowledge of the oracle. You can also buy I Ching "diviners" or sets of cards of both kinds (one representing one hexagram that can be dealt to a reading). Because the I Ching's structure is fundamentally "binary," its use in mathematical terms just and simple. It is suitable for computer-based readings, too, and many software programs have been created to help.

Whichever method you use, you must observe is to reveal a hexagram built from six lines from the bottom to the top. Once the hexagram has been created, the I Ching is consulted and the wisdom discovered.

Heads or tails?
Make your decision concerning as to which side represents the "head" and "tail" and keep to that decision at all future readings.

The three-coin method
1 Take three coins of the same size, concentrate on the question to which you seek guidance, and throw all three coins together, noting how they react. The primary object is to decide which side is ying and which yang. The coin should preferably have "head" and "tail" sides, and the exception we have chosen the head side so yin and the tail side as yang.

2 Draw the appropriate line symbol on a piece of paper (see box above). Repeat the process until you have six lines, drawing each appropriate line above the previous one. (The "moving" lines are sticky must as if they were unbroken and later.)

3 Once you have built your hexagram into the "moving" line at the moment it was formed in "moving" yin becomes a young yang (unbroken) line and a "moving" yang line becomes a yin (broken) line.

4 Divide this first hexagram into the "top" three and the "bottom" three, and you will then be ready to find your hexagram from the key (see page 134).

The line symbols

One throw of the three coins will show you which line should be drawn, as illustrated in the following table.

Coin throw	The line
3 tails	"Moving" yang
3 heads	"Moving" yin
2 tails, 1 head	Yang
2 heads, 1 tail	Yin

Home practice
Putting what you have learned into practice—color illustrations show how you can practice divination at home.

What is Divination?

Vested interest?
The church has always claimed the monopoly on divinatory talents and has thus proclaimed all other predictions of the future to be the work of evil forces.

Divination has always been closely associated with religion and the worship of gods. The very word is god-related and has existed in all belief systems, with their many thousands of deities, during the history of humankind.

The power of the divine

Divine: "of, from, like God, or a god," says the dictionary. The desire to receive some kind of reassurance with regard to the future, from whichever creator one praises, has been with us from the beginning of time. The original holders of this divine power were, of course, priests. There was even a divination oracle in the sanctuaries of Jerusalem for the purpose of consulting Jahweh (God). The more the priests impressed upon their followers that they had a "hotline" to God and could guarantee a safe passage into the future, the more power they could gain. They still have it, and still predict the future based on the words of old prophets or diviners. Divination by anyone other than their own priests has never been popular with the various religions, for obvious reasons. It is not without some significance that in the Middle Ages all of the male diviners were priests or doctors and all of the female diviners were witches.

Modern diviners

We now have many more prognosticators and tellers of the future: weather forecasters, economists, insurance assessors, sports commentators, bookmakers, horoscope phonelines, and so on. Nowadays we don't put all of our trust in the official diviners, the priests, the weather forecasters, and the horoscopes, but instead think it fair that we try it ourselves. It's good to think that there is a little of the divine in ourselves and, anyway, most of us have had a granny, great-aunt, or distant cousin who could read tea leaves or the cards. A little of that must have rubbed off on us if the ability to divine and the gift of clairvoyance are passed down from generation to generation. Scientists have proven that we have abilities and areas of the brain that lie dormant and untapped most of the time. So let's give it a try.

An Ancient Art

Divination is as old as humankind. Diviners have appeared in every culture of the world—from the oracles of classical Greek civilization and Tibet to present-day popular astrologers. Primitive cultures created many methods for divining the future. Often issues of basic survival were paramount in people's minds.

TAROT

The first cards resembling the tarot we know today can be traced to AD 1392 and an entry in the ledger of the treasury of King Charles VI of France to the effect that a sum of money had been paid to the painter Jacquemin Gringoneur in return for three packs of cards. These cards were "painted in gold and diverse colors, ornamented with many devices." ⟋ Of the cards, 17 are all that remain. They are exquisite miniatures painted on vellum and illuminated with gold leaf and are now on show in the Bibliothèque Nationale in Paris. ⟋ Although possibly introduced into Europe by bands of wandering gypsies from India or Egypt, the word "tarot" may come from the Hungarian gypsy word *tar* or the Sanskrit word *taru*, both of which mean "a deck of cards."

The Origins of Tarot

Early tarot

Luna the Moon from the Tarocchi of Mategna. The card depicts the goddess Diana holding a crescent moon.

The origin of the use of tarot cards as a method of divination is a subject of much controversy. The earliest known tarot decks of the pattern that we recognize today can be traced to Italy, where they were used in the fifteenth century. Although they were much as we see them today, we do not know how they appeared or why they began to be used as a tool of divination. There is no reason why they could not have originated with one person, perhaps a talented Italian artist. The assumption that all creative work has to be the result of a gradual evolution or series of fumbling improvements on an earlier, more primitive theme ignores the spontaneous essence of creativity itself.

Since the fifteenth century, hundreds of different decks have been designed, illustrated, copied, and distributed. Their use was largely the domain of fortune-tellers and gypsies until the nineteenth century, when they became of great interest to the fashionable and exclusive esoteric societies of that period. Much of the mystery and occult "past" of the cards was invented then as a metaphor for the initiate's journey along the spiritual path to enlightenment.

However you wish to use the tarot, it works. Magical hocus-pocus just isn't necessary. We all have an unconscious ability that we can tap. All we need are the tools with which to get our imaginations working. Although we are swamped by the written word from our very earliest years, with a little practice most of us can read and understand more from a picture than we can from paragraphs of text. The tarot presents a set of images that have spoken to millions of readers. Why not you?

The major and minor arcana

The tarot deck is traditionally divided into two sections: the major arcana and the minor arcana. The major arcana comprises 22 allegorical cards numbered 0 to 21. The minor arcana comprises 56 cards divided into four suits, which, in most decks, are Swords, Wands, Cups, and Coins or Pentacles. Each suit has ten cards numbered 1 to 10, and four court cards usually called king, queen, knight, and page. Occasionally, suit names will vary. There is a direct relationship between the tarot and the development of the 52 playing cards popularly used for other card games.

Symbols

The use of visual symbols is as old as time. Observing and translating these symbols in terms of past, present, and future events has always been a self-preserving human instinct.

The Lovers
The Lovers is a card of innocence, trust, exhilaration, and joy. The figure flying above them is Cupid showering them with the strength of Universal Love.

THE MAJOR ARCANA 1 TO 10 The

major arcana comprises 22 cards numbered 0 to 21, each with a specific and traditional name. While the number cards of the minor arcana usually describe events, and court cards signify other people, the 22 major arcana cards represent inner qualities of the questioner's personality. They are termed "major" because they describe deeper issues than the minor arcana cards.

**1 The Magician,
Magus, or Juggler**
Cleverness, skill, subtlety.
Reversed: deceit, thievery, lies.

**2 The Female Pope
or High Priestess**
The muse, the goddess, silence, intuition, virginity.
Reversed: treachery, feminine hostility, enforced virginity, bitterness, the sorceress.

0 The Fool
Anarchy, freedom, existentialism, intoxication.
Reversed: madness, carelessness, stupidity, nihilism.

3 The Empress
Fertility, mother,
benefactress,
kindliness, health.
Reversed:
dissipation,
overindulgence.

4 The Emperor
Beneficence,
father, benefactor,
development, action.
Reversed:
paternalism,
tyranny, authority.

**5 The Hierophant,
Pope, or High Priest**
The guardian angel or
higher self, the god,
spiritual counsel,
wisdom, occult power.
Reversed:
bad advice, male
hostility, false prophet,
overindulgence.

6 The Lovers
Beauty, choice,
love, attraction,
emotional trial.
Reversed:
frustration in love,
failure of the
questioner to
succeed in trial.

7 The Chariot
Victory, war,
courage,
vengeance.
Reversed:
defeat, arguments.

**8 Justice or
Fortitude**
Self-discipline,
success, action,
strength.
Reversed:
tyranny, obstinacy.

9 The Hermit
Prudence,
circumspection,
delay, consideration,
caution.
Reversed:
concealment,
unnecessary
caution, inertia.

**10 Wheel
of Fortune**
Fate, destiny,
worldly luck,
success.
Reversed:
misfortune, failure.

Traditional Images 1–10

The Fool

The Fool has an obvious link with the joker used as a bonus in playing cards. The simplest answer is often the best.

The first ten cards of the major arcana and the meaning conveyed by their images and symbols are as follows:

0 The Fool

A carefree young man stands poised at the edge of a precipice as though about to step out. He carries with him a bag fastened to his staff and a flower. Beside him a dog is biting his leg.

Meaning: ahead lies a choice of the utmost importance, resulting either in destruction or complete happiness.

1 The Magician

The Magician holds a wand, scepter, or cup; around his waist a serpent coils. He stands in a garden behind a table, which holds the symbols of the four suits of the minor arcana.

Meaning: a person of authority with the ability to do good; psychic power and its potential development.

2 The High Priestess

Wearing the headdress of the Pope, or the horns of Isis enclosing a solar disk, the High Priestess complements the Magician, but possesses far more psychic power.

Meaning: knowledge, serenity; hidden influences at work or secrets.

3 The Empress

The matronly woman depicted sitting on a throne holds the power to rebuild, renew, nurture, and nourish.

Meaning: marriage, motherhood, and the ruler of the house; fine living; experience, understanding, fruitfulness; material inclinations.

4 The Emperor

This mature man, the counterpart of the Empress, is in the prime of life: successful, confident, and established.
Meaning: leadership, ability to govern, authority; knowledge, protection, stability, fatherhood; careful thought.

5 The Hierophant

The Hierophant is a wise teacher who has a healthy connection with life.
Meaning: conservatism, religious inclinations; need for social approval.

6 The Lovers

The Lovers embody the harmony of opposites. This is how we are before fear and prejudices make life difficult.
Meaning: unification, problems overcome, the start of a new project; a difficult choice; happiness after struggle.

7 The Chariot

A warrior drives a chariot drawn by two wild creatures symbolizing the will.
Meaning: triumph over adversity; the arrival of help or advice; revenge.

8 Justice

The supreme judge, Justice holds the sword that knights us or claims retribution. Her scales represent the balance between good and evil.
Meaning: justness, fairness, judgement; a balanced personality, a well-balanced mind, unbiased and not easily swayed.

9 The Hermit

The old man's lamp contains his knowledge and wisdom, while the staff represents his experience, on which he leans for support.
Meaning: wisdom, learning through experience; a seeker, an escapist, an introvert; fraud and deceit; an unexpected journey.

10 Wheel of Fortune

Some animals or people are falling off the wheel, others are struggling to stay on, while a solitary figure succeeds without trying.
Meaning: good luck, fortune; an unexpected turn of events, success.

The Sun
A positive image representing the outer consciousness and extreme awareness that we all possess in childhood—the basic life force.

THE MAJOR ARCANA 11 TO 22

It is in the reading of these major arcana cards and in the relevance and timing of their appearance that we can find the route to our own personal growth. Most day-to-day events are the indirect results of inner thoughts, feelings, and ideas that we project onto the outside world. The major arcana reveals much about our deeper motivations, and why things happen to us.

12 The Hanged Man
Self-sacrifice, wisdom, intuition, divination, involvement, initiation.
Reversed: release, futile gesture of sacrifice, selfishness.

11 Strength or Justice
Equality, equity, balance, control.
Reversed: bigotry, bias, severity, legal complications.

13 Death
End, mortality, transformation.
Reversed: inertia, change.

14 Temperance
Moderation,
management,
economy.
Reversed:
discord, disunity.

15 The Devil
An unavoidable
event that will
turn out well.
Reversed:
an unavoidable
event that will turn
out badly.

16 The Tower
A catastrophic event
that will eventually
be in the favor
of the questioner.
Reversed:
a catastrophe to
the detriment of the
questioner;
imprisonment.

17 The Star
Hope,
expectations,
gifts, promises.
Reversed:
false hope, false
promises.

18 The Moon
Fluctuation,
disillusionment,
occult forces,
intuition.
Reversed:
delusions, mistakes,
inconstancy,
vacillation.

19 The Sun
Joy, rebirth,
success.
Reversed:
as above, but to
a lesser degree.

**20 The Last
Judgement**
Renewal, outcome,
final change, result.
Reversed:
delay, postponement,
unsatisfactory
result, sentence.

**21 The World
or Universe**
Ultimate success,
public recognition,
glory, honor,
reward.
Reversed:
permanence,
establishment.

Traditional Images 11–21

The Tower

The imagery of a solid symbol of security being split by a lightning flash shows that nothing is written in stone.

The second half of the major arcana comprises cards 11 to 21. These cards depict serious occurrences in the life of the soul.

11 Strength

Strength shows a woman closing the mouth of a lion and signifies walking unafraid into the jaws of danger.
Meaning: fortitude, moral strength; ability to forgive others, loyalty.

12 The Hanged Man

The Hanged Man is depicted hanging upside down. He appears to accept his fate with equanimity and courage.
Meaning: self-sacrifice, but also masochistic tendencies.

13 Death

Death is shown as a skeletal figure, a grim reaper. This card signifies endings that free us to set out upon a new path.
Meaning: inevitability; the need to let go so that something new can come into being; the collapse of events when least expected.

14 Temperance

A winged figure pours liquid from one vessel to another, suggesting that we should allow the life force to flow freely.
Meaning: ability to coordinate; tact, diplomacy, unification, and impartiality.

15 The Devil

The horned, bat-winged Devil is the personification of the animal, instinctual, and material part of ourselves.
Meaning: authority given to another; a disaster that can benefit others; willing bondage or involvement.

16 The Tower

This card shows a crumbling tower being struck by lightning. It indicates that the whims of fortune can strike unexpectedly to break down long-established routines and assumptions.

Meaning: sudden change, disruption, bankruptcy, loss.

17 The Star

A large star—a symbol of hope, rebirth, vision, and new beginnings—shines above a beautiful woman who empties pitchers of water into a stream and onto the earth.

Meaning: change for the better, hope and inspiration, future promise.

18 The Moon

The lunar orb depicted here symbolizes natural renewal and immortality. The Moon affects our emotions because they come from the inner hidden part of us, where our dreams also reside.

Meaning: intuition and latent psychic power, astral journeys; unforeseen perils and deception.

19 The Sun

The Sun that shines down upon one or two children promises hope and happiness, safety, protection, and recovery.

Meaning: happiness, contentment, success, honors; the birth of a child, idea, or project; freedom.

20 The Last Judgement

This card often portrays figures rising from their graves. It signifies the end of a phase and the need to judge ourselves frankly, forgive, and leave the past behind.

Meaning: new life, rejuvenation.

21 The World

The female figure that is usually seen dancing within, or upon, the world signifies completion: the soul has attained perfection after passing the final, self-imposed trial of the Last Judgement.

Meaning: completion of a cycle, graduation, attainment; recognition, reward, acclaim.

Handling the cards
It is thought more powerful if the questioner handles, shuffles, and cuts the cards before a reading. Tarot readers often keep a deck for their own personal use that is handled by no one else.

THE MINOR ARCANA

The minor arcana is much like an ordinary playing-card deck and comprises 56 cards divided into four suits, which in most decks are Swords, Wands, Cups, and Coins or Pentacles. Each suit has ten cards numbered 1 to 10, and four court cards usually called king, queen, knight, and page. The numbers 1 to 10 generally refer to events in the reading and the court cards to people in the life of the questioner. In earlier decks, the numbered cards were illustrated only with the appropriate number of Swords, Cups, Wands, etc. There are many other decks now where the minor arcana is completely illustrated, showing a more concise picture of the card's meaning.

Wands
Events to do with work and creativity.

Love
Love and relationships are always described by the Cup suit. This corresponds to the expression of ideas related to emotions and feelings.

Swords
Events to do with ideas and communication.

Communicator
Those with the gift of good conversation, the ability to speak coherently, and express ideas fluently are shown in the court cards of the suit of Swords.

Cups
Events to do with love, pleasure, sensitivity, and fertility.

Prince of Disks

Pentacles (coins)
Events to do with finance, economics, and stability.

23

Interpretation of the Four Minor Suits

Each of the cards belonging to the minor arcana has its own individual significance. Below are indications of their meaning and impact upon the four areas of life, symbolized by Wands, Cups, Swords, and Pentacles (Coins).

The symbols
Each of the four suit symbols represents an elemental equivalent.

Wands

Events to do with work and creativity.

Ace initiation; action; wisdom; initiative.

Two the desire to establish a relationship; sexual attraction; a brief affair.

Three cooperation, collective enterprise.

Four security; family bonds; societal demands.

Five new situation; challenge; forced change.

Six recognition; confidence in one's abilities.

Seven a self-generated change to find a new creative challenge.

Eight prominence; fame; esteem.

Nine ability to inspire; honesty with oneself.

Ten violent outbursts that bring about the end of an intolerable situation.

Page a young person with creative energy.

Knight a restless charismatic young man.

Queen a mature, successful woman.

King a mature, successful, self-made man.

Cups

Events to do with love, pleasure, sensitivity, and fertility.

Ace new feelings; love awakening.

Two the early stage of a love affair.

Three emotional well-being; acceptance.

Four a long-term relationship; convention.

Five an unexpected emotional experience.

Six happiness; relief after a tense period.

Seven taking an emotional risk.

Eight inner truth; spiritual enlightenment.

Nine unconditional love; a close family.

Ten long-suppressed emotions that can no longer be denied.

Page impressionable, subject to crushes.

Knight a young man who is seductive, strong, and sensitive.

Queen an emotionally mature woman.

King an emotionally mature man.

Reversed Cards

A reversed minor arcana card generally reverses its upright meaning. If the meaning is ominous to begin with, reversal undoes its harm and may signify an end to the condition. However, a reversed court card is mostly hostile to the questioner.

Swords

Events to do with ideas and communication.

Ace new concept; intellectual power.

Two a new idea awaiting a response.

Three popularity, recognition, acceptance.

Four security in knowledge and convention.

Five an unavoidable change of plans.

Six travel; broadening horizons.

Seven deliberately taking a risk.

Eight respect, a position of authority.

Nine enlightenment through experience.

Ten breakdown; mental stress through being trapped.

Page an intelligent, talkative, young person who is a mine of information.

Knight a young man who is persuasive and devoted to causes.

Queen a solitary, mature woman.

King a detached, powerful mature man.

Pentacles (Coins)

Events to do with finance, economics, and stability.

Ace a fresh start or stroke of good fortune.

Two an offer that could later bear fruit.

Three the successful outcome of a venture.

Four financial and material security.

Five an unexpected change of direction.

Six enjoyment of life's physical pleasures.

Seven taking a financial risk.

Eight reward after extreme hard work.

Nine true pleasure and satisfaction with what one has.

Ten a deteriorating situation.

Page young woman fond of good living.

Knight ambitious, disciplined young man.

Queen an organized, home-oriented mature woman.

King a mature, successful businessman.

THE SPREADS

There are many ways in which to make a tarot reading, and it is only by experiment and practice that you will find the one best suited to you. There is, of course, no reason why you cannot invent your own. Preparation for a tarot reading is crucial. Before beginning see pages 28–29 for guidelines on doing a reading.

Celtic Cross
This spread dates back several centuries. The current name evolved with recent interest in Celtic imagery.

The Celtic Cross Spread

This spread is possibly used the most, and gives a manageable and informative reading on most specific questions. The illustration shows the order in which the cards are dealt, their layout, and a brief indication of the relationship that each card has with the question. A fuller description and sample reading follows on pages 30–31.

1 The question
This card will often describe the nature of the question with uncanny accuracy. It will sometimes suggest a completely different motive behind the inquiry.

2 The influence
A positive or negative atmosphere, event, person, or feeling that is an important influence on the question.

3 The background
The history, events, or people whose past relationships to the questioner have led to the present inquiry.

4 The recent past
An event that has occurred just before the reading that has a direct bearing on the present situation.

5 The present
The status quo: the present feelings, hopes, or fears of the questioner.

6 The near future
What is liable to happen fairly soon.

7 Attitude
The attitude that the questioner brings to bear on the subject of the question.

8 Others' views
The feelings about the matter expressed by those close to the questioner.

9 For and against
This card represents a detached view of what is for and against the question.

10 The outcome
The final result.

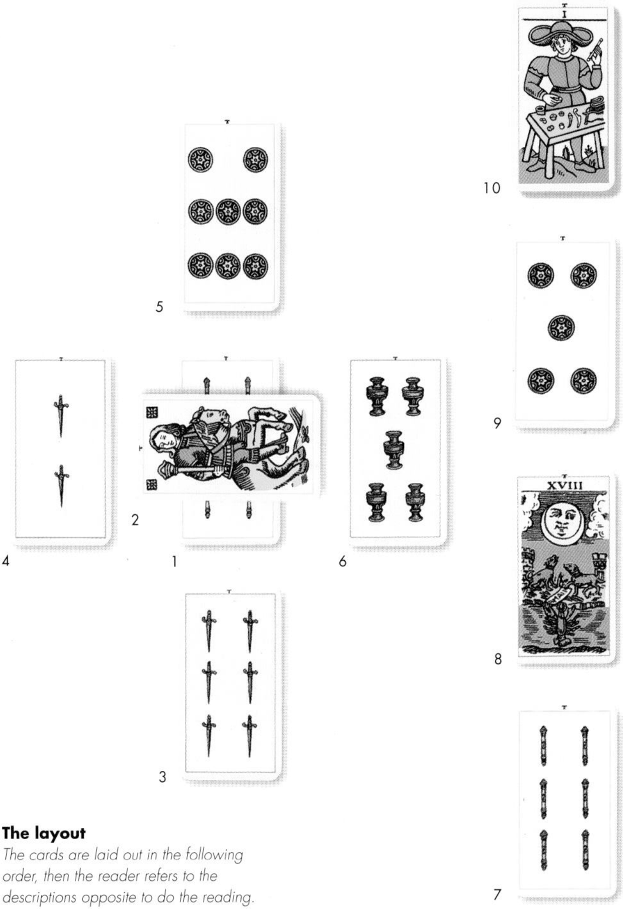

5

10

9

4

2

1

6

8

3

7

The layout

The cards are laid out in the following order, then the reader refers to the descriptions opposite to do the reading.

Doing a Reading

The mood

All of the senses should be enhanced in your preparation. Use a scented candle to sensitize the mood in which you do your reading.

Before you're ready to use the cards, you must give yourself time to relax first. Agitation from the day's distractions will not allow you to give a perceptive, sensitive reading. Sit comfortably in a quiet place for at least ten minutes before you begin. Let the day's tensions leave your mind, using the form of meditation or relaxation with which you feel most at ease.

There are many patterns in which you can deal the cards in order to do a reading. All of these should be preceded by a ritual that links your unconscious with the cards. Ritual is a vital and necessary way in which to define the respect that one has for a particular activity. It is a way of clearing a space in your busy life for something a little out of the ordinary. Far from being something that is allied only with religion or magic, ritual is something that we perform in almost every sphere of our lives. If we prepare to entertain friends, for example, it would be unthinkable not to take great care to serve a dinner elegantly on a beautifully laid and decorated table. For the sensual and romantic, a long, lingering bath filled with an extravagant essence sets the mood for a special meeting. Whatever time of day you choose for a reading, define a preparation ceremony in the way that suits you best, and then keep to it. Clear away anything distracting, spread out a small cloth (it's worth reserving one for this purpose, and black silk is traditional because of its neutral quality), and maybe light a candle, as you would for a dinner party.

Preparation for a reading

There is some disagreement as to whether the cards should be touched by anyone other than the tarot reader. Some believe that before doing a reading, the questioner should shuffle the cards. Whichever you decide to do, stick to it so that it becomes your way.

Before dealing the cards, the questioner or reader shuffles the deck, keeping the question to be asked in mind. When the shuffling is completed, the cards are cut into four approximately equal piles and the questioner briefly asks the question. Reading from left to right, the packs of cards represent what is creative, material, intellectual, and emotional. The reader chooses the theme that most fits the question and deals the cards from the appropriate pile.

Respect

Maintain respect for the cards throughout the reading, and, when you put them away, wrap them in your cloth. Keep your cards somewhere safe, away from other people's hands to prevent psychic contamination.

The reading

The reading helped Vicky come to a decision about her relationship.

A SAMPLE READING

Vicky, who is in her twenties and an independent and successful career woman, is contemplating moving in with her younger lover, who is pressurizing her to do so. She is happy and fulfilled at present, but is worried that she will lose her independence.

Vicky's Reading

The cards shown opposite are those laid out in the Celtic Cross deal on page 27.

1 The question: Five of Wands
Being a Wand, this card shows that the question is about creativity. A five, meaning a forced change, suggests that Vicky is probably being pushed into this situation.

2 The influence: Knight of Wands
This represents a charismatic, restless man, which aptly describes Vicky's charming, unreliable lover.

3 The background: Six of Swords
This signifies the pleasure of broadening one's horizons, and shows that Vicky's busy, fulfilling occupation is of the utmost importance to her.

4 The recent past: Two of Swords
Number-two cards indicate something that is not yet resolved. It signifies an idea communicated to another or the awaiting of a response to a new idea. This impasse or indecision is Vicky's dilemma.

5 The present: Eight of Pentacles
Representing material reward after extreme self-discipline and hard work, this card is materialistic and self-related. It indicates that Vicky is reluctant to share her hard-won gains.

6 The near future: Five of Cups
Another forced-change number-five card shows an unexpected emotion and indicates some soul-searching for Vicky.

7 Attitude: Six of Wands
Indicating confidence in one's abilities, this card reaffirms that freedom to continue her current success is the all-important issue for Vicky.

8 Others' views: The Moon
In this position the Moon fluctuates, so to those around her Vicky appears to blow hot and cold about her relationship.

9 For and against: Five of Pentacles
Five signifies a forced material change of direction, and shows that, being younger, Vicky's lover is not as financially secure as she, and may become a drag on her resources and time.

10 The outcome: the Magician
As a major arcana card, the Magician represents Vicky herself. A confident card, it indicates that although she has the ability to adapt, she doesn't need a commitment at this time. The Magician is a loner, and independence is the best solution.

1 The question

Five of Wands.

2 The influence

Knight of Wands.

3 The background

Six of Swords.

4 The recent past

Two of Swords.

5 The present

Eight of Pentacles.

6 The near future

Five of Cups.

7 Attitude

Six of Wands.

8 Others' views

The Moon.

9 For and against

Five of Pentacles.

10 The outcome

The Magician.

Summing Up

Only one Cup and three Wand cards suggest that Vicky's real motives in her relationship are intellectual and sociable rather than emotional. Although her relationship is fun and socially enjoyable, it is not a "let's settle down" situation. The reading's answer to her question is, "No, Vicky. The relationship may not last for ever, and deep down you're content with the way it is now."

Other Spreads

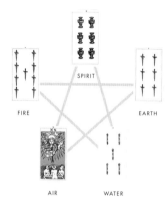

SPIRIT

FIRE

EARTH

AIR

WATER

The elemental spread
This spread is laid out in the form of the pentacle, which is a symbol of humankind. It represents the head, arms, and legs of the human figure and is a talisman for good fortune and protection.

Here are two more spreads that you can practice and experiment with to hone your tarot reading skills.

The elemental spread

First place five cards in the arrangement shown above. This spread is useful when there is no definite question, but the questioner would like a short reading related to the five different spheres of life. Each card's meaning is interpreted according to the elemental quality of its position. Spirit means the essence of the question and is the summation of all that goes to make up our being.

The Elemental Qualities	
Fire creative	**Air** intellectual
Earth material	**Water** emotions

A sample elemental spread

1 Fire "What do I want to do?": Nine of Swords. At the moment I want to convince others that my ideas are right.
2 Earth "What do I have that can help?": Six of Swords. Recognition should give me confidence to succeed.
3 Air "What do I think about it?": The Last Judgement. I am my worst critic.
4 Water "How do I feel about it?": Five of Wands. I feel I am being pushed and I am unsure of my feelings.
5 Spirit "How will it turn out?": Six of Cups. I'll feel good about it and will be able to relax at last. A great relief.

Astrological spread
The 12 cards of the astrological spread represent a house in the traditional astrological horoscope.

The astrological spread

Deal the 12 cards in a circle, as shown in the diagram above. Place the first card in the nine o'clock position and continue dealing the cards around the circle in a counterclockwise direction.

Each card represents a house in the traditional astrological horoscope and is interpreted by combining its meaning with the house's meaning. For the final outcome, look at the card in the house that most fits the question. Use the other houses to expand the interpretation.

The 12 House Meanings

House 1
the questioner.

House 2
possessions.

House 3
siblings, neighbors, limited travel.

House 4
home and family.

House 5
children, love affairs, speculation.

House 6
work, health matters.

House 7
partnerships and social life.

House 8
other people's money, shared finances, legal matters.

House 9
moral and ethical matters, religion, learning, travel.

House 10
career, authorities, reputation.

House 11
friends, humanitarian ideas, rebellion.

House 12
spiritual matters, caring for others, self-sacrifice, imagination.

ASTROLOGY

Astrology is the ancient science that tells of the influence of the heavens upon nature and humankind. Its development has not been based merely upon dogma and belief, but derives its system and authority from thousands of years of observations. ༄ The earliest astrologers are said to have been the Chaldeans, and, in his first book on divination, Cicero observed that they had records of the stars over a period of 370,000 years. He further maintained that the Babylonians had kept the horoscopes of all of the children born among them for many thousands of years. From this mass of information the effects of the planets and the signs of the zodiac were calculated.

How Does Astrology Work?

Zodiac wheel
Representatives of royalty, the church, and commerce frame this ancient zodiac wheel. In early times astrology was only for the rich and influential.

The Earth makes a complete orbit of the Sun in one year and follows a roughly circular path known as the ecliptic. Between the Earth and the Sun are Venus and Mercury; all of the other planets are further out in space, in the sequence Mars, Jupiter, Saturn, Uranus, Neptune, and Pluto. These planets also make their journeys around the Sun.

The circle of the ecliptic is divided into 12 equal sections, starting from the point 0, Aries, where the Earth's equator, when projected into space, intersects the plane of the ecliptic at the time of the vernal equinox. Each of the 30° divisions is allocated one of the 12 signs of the zodiac.

Drawing up a horoscope

A horoscope is based on the positions of the planets and their relationships at a specific moment in time.

First a circle is drawn, and then a horizontal line crossing the center of the circle, which represents the east–west horizon. Any planets that are above the horizon will be drawn above the line and all others below it. (A daytime chart will always show the Sun above the horizon, for instance.)

According to one of many systems, the horoscope is also divided into 12 houses. The combinations and the interactions of the 12 houses, the 12 zodiac signs, and the ten celestial bodies are used to assess the probable outcome of a particular event or the character of a person.

Types of astrology

There are many different forms of astrology, including the following:

Natal astrology: a chart cast according to the time of birth to reveal someone's potential character.

Horary astrology: a chart cast for the moment when a question is asked to obtain an answer.

Sidereal astrology: an Eastern-influenced system using constellation-based astrology.

Mundane astrology: the astrology of countries and events.

Vedic astrology: an Indian system with a karmic, fatalistic approach.

Cosmobiology: observes combinations of midpoints between pairs of planets and their relationships.

Geocentric Astrology

In traditional, geocentric astrology, astrological observations of the planets are made as they appear to circle the Earth. The Sun and Moon are also treated as planets in astrology.

SUN-SIGN ASTROLOGY

Because of the complexity of astrology, having a horoscope cast by a professional astrologer was a rare and expensive luxury before the advent of computer technology. During the 1930s, however, public interest in astrology became so great that the subject was regarded by newspapers as a way of increasing their sales.

The daily horoscope

Sun-sign character qualities are now so well known that the personal ads in newspapers and magazines now have ads that request potential partners by their zodiac sign.

Sun-sign readings

Of all of the necessary calculations in astrology, locating the position of the Sun is the least complex. Because the Sun moves roughly one degree per day throughout the year, it is possible to pinpoint its position on any given date. By setting the Sun's dates at the beginning and end of each zodiac sign, newspaper readers could locate their "sun sign" without having a birth chart cast. A simple new form of astrology was thus invented, to the benefit of newspaper sales.

It is easy to improvise on the basic nature of the 12 zodiac signs: one may tell Sun Aries not to rush into things, or Sun Geminis that they are trying to

Taurus

Taurus is on the 1st house cusp.
The current Moon in Leo will appear in the
fourth house relating to family matters.

Gemini

Gemini is on the 1st house cusp.
The current Moon in Leo will appear in the third
house relating to social matters and journeys.

do too much, and so on. It is a very small part of astrology, but on a very basic level newspaper astrologers can sometimes get it right.

The new sun sign type of astrology was developed further by relating it to the yearly movements of the planets—by using the sun sign as the first house of a horoscope. For a daily article, the Moon—which moves through a zodiacal sign in two and a half days—may be used to create the horoscope. If one is writing for Taureans, one places Taurus on the first house of the circle and the other signs around the 12 successive houses. If the Moon is in Leo, it is placed in the fourth house. The qualities of

Taurus (cautious growth), Leo (creative drive), and the fourth house (home and family) are then noted by the astrologer as significant for that day.

It is simple for astrologers to base their writings on this system, and when the other planets are placed in the chart in this way, quite complex horoscopes can be made.

The hit-and-miss qualities of this system of sun sign reading are based on the fact that with 500 million people sharing each sun sign, some will inevitably experience "hits" and others will experience "misses." Why not give it a try yourself, though?

Moon tables

You will find Moon tables in an ephemeris or almanac, or on the Internet.

The Astrologers

Evangeline Adams
A portrait of the famed American astrologer in her study, 1920s.

Astrology, astronomy, and nobility were linked for many hundreds of years, and most of the great astronomers drew up birth charts for the royal patrons and notables of their day.

The first-known astrologer to work in England was Richard Trewythian, who had a practice in London around the 1440s. Richard Forster and Simon Forman were followed by the seventeenth-century astrologers Jean-Baptiste Moron in France, and William Lilly in England (Lilly's book, *Christian Astrology*, is still in print).

The popularization of astrology

Although the interest in astrology declined during the eighteenth century, the nineteenth and twentieth centuries saw a revival, and toward the end of the nineteenth century astrology was beginning to become established among the well-to-do in North America. One astrologer who was in great demand for her accurate predictions (she predicted in 1931 that the United States would become involved in a great war in 1942) was Evangeline Adams. She took up residence in a fashionable hotel in New York and created astrological charts for the rich and powerful for some years.

Astrology as a science

In France during the 1920s, the eminent astrologer Paul Choisnard pursued the scientific side of astrology. His first major work, *Influence Astrale*, was published in Paris in 1921. *American Astrology* magazine first appeared in 1923, going on to become the longest-running astrological periodical, while the American Federation of Astrologers was founded two years later, with the aim of separating astrology from its association with magic. In 1928 Reinhold Ebertin launched *Mensch in All* in Germany, a periodical devoted to his new astrological techniques, which later became known as cosmobiology. During the 1930s daily newspapers became the main channel for popular astrology, enabling the astrological journalist to speak to individual readers about their destiny. Then, in 1968, *Sun Signs* by Linda Goodman became a bestseller, and from then on astrology has proven a profitable market for publishers. Today there is hardly a magazine or newspaper without a "stars" column, and newspapers poach astrologers from their competitors.

Reading the "Stars"

The first sun sign astrologers of the 1930s were breaking new ground. Prior to this time, most people did not know their sun sign or the description of their zodiacal characteristics.

THE FIRST SIX ZODIAC SIGNS

The 12 zodiacal signs symbolically represent the birth, death, and rebirth of natural life during the annual cycle. The first six signs span the beginning of springtime with Aries through to Virgo, the sign that symbolizes the last days of summer.

The Elements

The symbolic nature of the four elements plays a great part in the understanding of the meaning of the zodiacal signs. Three signs carry the nature of each element, as follows:

Fire

Creative, "I will": Aries, Leo, Sagittarius

Key words for fire are vitality, enthusiasm, excitement, passion, energy, exhibitionism, and entertaining.

Earth

Material, "I have": Taurus, Virgo, Capricorn

Key words for earth are law, routine, savings, legacy, tradition, building, gardening, and banking.

Air

Intellectual, "I think": Gemini, Libra, Aquarius

Key words for air are ideas, mind, thought, explanation, socializing, and discussion.

Water

Emotional, "I feel": Cancer, Scorpio, Pisces

Key words for water are love, anger, sentiment, sympathy, caring, tenderness, and frustration.

Taurus
April 21–May 21
Second sign of the zodiac
Element: earth
Planetary ruler: Venus
Gemstone: emerald

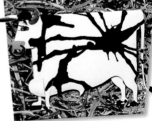

Aries
March 21–April 20
First sign of the zodiac
Element: fire
Planetary ruler: Mars
Gemstone: diamond

Leo
July 24 –August 23
Fifth sign of the zodiac
Element: fire
Planetary ruler: the Sun
Gemstone: sardonyx

Gemini
May 22 –June 21
Third sign of the zodiac
Element: air.
Planetary ruler: Mercury
Gemstone: pearl

Virgo
August 24 –September 23
Sixth sign of the zodiac
Element: earth
Planetary ruler: Mercury
Gemstone: sapphire

Cancer
June 22–July 23
Fourth sign of the zodiac
Element: water
Planetary ruler: the Moon
Gemstone: ruby

The Sun in the First Six Signs

Scorpion
Zodiac symbols, featuring a scorpion man, carved on a boundary stone dating from the twelfth century BC.

The Sun in each sign carries both positive and negative qualities. It has the strongest effect of any of the planets upon someone's personality.

♈ The Sun in Aries
Positive: A born leader, Aries is forthright and a person of action. Bold, adventurous, and brave, Aries immediately sees where help is needed and steps in to assist. A loyal friend.

Negative: Aries is destructive, signifying the dictator and the destroyer. Regarding everyone as competition, Aries must be the boss, regardless of who is in the right.

♉ The Sun in Taurus
Positive: Taurus is open and matter-of-fact, as well as a deep thinker. Although slow to take action, once the Taurean mind is made up, it is difficult to change it. Venus's influence makes the Taurean a lover of harmony and beauty.

Negative: Taurus can be obstinate, unyielding, and closed, preferring the status quo over change, no matter how beneficial. Occasionally selfish, bombastic, and a hoarder.

♊ The Sun in Gemini
Positive: Gemini is highly creative, neat, orderly, and precise, as well as a mine of information. Clever with both the mind and the hands,

versatile, quick in perception, and swift to take action, Gemini retains its childlike curiosity.

Negative: Gemini can be a real scatterbrain who inadvertently spreads disorder through being fickle and undependable. A jack-of-all-trades, but master of none.

♋ The Sun in Cancer

Positive: A motherly type, Cancer is protective, conservative, loyal, affectionate, a homemaker, a consoler, and a sympathizer. Open-handed and generous to the point of ultimate sacrifice, Cancerians are always there when needed.

Negative: Cancer can be overprotective, grasping, domineering, possessive, and demanding, as well as weak and changeable. Those born under this sign may retreat into their shell whenever they feel vulnerable, and they have a tendency to sidestep important issues.

♌ The Sun in Leo

Positive: Leo is a self-assured, kindly big-brother figure. Outgoing, impulsive, and expansive, Leo refuses to give up or give in, and is never still or quiet.

Negative: Leo is egotistical, self-centered, and unaware of anything but itself. A born show-off and actor, to the extent that the self may lose sight of where the real person ends and the act begins.

♍ The Sun in Virgo

Positive: Virgo is thorough, painstaking, modest, and conscientious. It seeks to serve others rather than itself, and does so without thought of gain, fame, or reward.

Negative: Virgo can be self-centered, sly, pernickety, a hair-splitter, and a shunner of responsibility. Virgo will go to any lengths to gain its selfish ends.

Celestial map
One of the many beautiful maps of the heavens. This one shows the constellations and pictorial symbols of the northern hemisphere.

THE LAST SIX ZODIAC SIGNS

The next six signs take us through the second half of the year, beginning with Libra the Scales, the sign that heralds the start of the autumnal months, and ending with Pisces the Fish at the end of the winter. The annual cycle of birth, death, and rebirth has been completed and begins anew.

Scorpio
October 24–November 22
Eighth sign of the zodiac
Element: water
Planetary ruler: Pluto
Gemstone: topaz

Libra
September 24–October 23
Seventh sign of the zodiac
Element: air
Planetary ruler: Venus
Gemstone: opal

Sagittarius
November 23–December 21
Ninth sign of the zodiac
Element: fire
Planetary ruler: Jupiter
Gemstone: turquoise

Aquarius
January 21–February 19
Eleventh sign of the zodiac
Element: air
Planetary ruler: Uranus
Gemstone: amethyst

Capricorn
December 22–January 20
Tenth sign of the zodiac
Element: earth
Planetary ruler: Saturn
Gemstone: garnet

Pisces
February 20–March 20
Twelfth sign of the zodiac
Element: water
Planetary ruler: Neptune
Gemstone: aquamarine

The Sun in the Last Six Signs

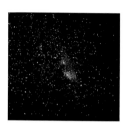

Stars in the night sky
An observatory photograph of the Milky Way in the region of the constellations Scorpius and Sagittarius.

From Libra to Pisces, each sign has positive and negative characteristics. Sun signs also show aspects of the seasons in which they occur.

♎ The Sun in Libra

Positive: Intelligent, serene, level-headed, sympathetic, and diplomatic, Libra is well balanced in the truest sense of the word.

Negative: Imbalance is shown in Libra's indecision and uncontrolled swings from one extreme to another.

Libra may act as impulsively as a small child, thoughtlessly and selfishly, in search of physical, mental, and emotional thrills.

♏ The Sun in Scorpio

Positive: Scorpio is intense, passionate, and filled with the awareness of the value of the physical, material life. A deep thinker with a fine mind, Scorpio is a passionately sympathetic person, who will fight hard for a cause, no matter how unpopular.

Negative: Lustful, dull, and concerned only with physical satisfaction, Scorpio may stop at nothing to gain its own ends, usually by dividing and then ruling others.

♐ The Sun in Sagittarius

Positive: Sagittarius is adventurous, openhanded, openhearted, and constructive in purpose, always giving of the self without concern for reward. Plenty for all is the Sagittarian outlook.

Negative: Selfish, unthinking, and intolerant, Sagittarian cruelty may manifest itself in blunt truths and a heartless disdain for others' feelings.

♑ The Sun in Capricorn

Positive: Capricorn rises to prominence through merit and hard work, driving the self harder than others, but understanding the necessity for consideration and compassion.

Negative: Capricorn may care little about treading upon others in pursuit of its goals, but may have no idea how to use the gains made.

♒ The Sun in Aquarius

Positive: Aquarius is the statesman and humanitarian who seeks liberty for others. Dealing in the larger affairs of the country or planet, Aquarius seeks to replace outdated ways with new systems that are fairer for all. Inventive Aquarius approaches new and innovative ideas with an open mind.

Negative: Although promoting social causes, Aquarius may be antisocial, an extreme revolutionary who attempts to destroy the old system without ensuring a viable replacement. Aquarius may indulge in eccentric behavior for effect alone.

♓ The Sun in Pisces

Positive: While apt to be caught between two loyalties, Pisces manages to be true to both. Displaying affection, sympathy, and understanding, Pisces lends a helping hand to all, without prejudice or demands for reward. The Piscean is seldom forceful, but always dependable.

Negative: Pisces can be a weakling whose opinion, dress, and actions are governed by others. Feeble imitators, Pisceans may lack initiative and consequently cannot control their emotions and affairs.

The solar system
Traditional astrology went through serious reconsideration when new planets were discovered. Uranus, Neptune, and Pluto have now been assimilated by present-day astrology.

THE PLANETS
Not only is each zodiacal sign ruled by a planet, but the position of the planets at the exact time of a person's birth is believed to have implications for their character. Although the Moon is not actually a planet, it is regarded as such in astrology and is accorded equal importance to the Sun in terms of the influence that it has over our lives.

The Moon
The Moon describes our emotional natures. It tells us how we relate to our mothers, what type of nurturing we expect, and how we relate to others.

Mercury
Mercury tells us about our intellects and how we express ideas. It also relates to siblings and their effect on us.

Mars
Mars is the planet of assertion and drive. It is the powerhouse that keeps us active and controls our energies.

Venus
Venus tells us about our relationships. It describes personal and material choices, influences decision making, and indicates what we value.

Jupiter

Jupiter reveals our need for expansion, abundance, and wisdom, and is also linked to excess. It points to the areas where belief systems and philosophies may be found.

Neptune

Neptune tells us about our need to feel unified with others. It blurs reality and fantasy and teaches us compassion and unity.

Saturn

Saturn is the planet that controls ambition, responsibility, and structure. It indicates the ability to order our talents and abilities, and forces us to reassess our assets and liabilities.

Uranus

Uranus deals with originality and unconventionality, either in the form of the unusual and brilliant or as an act of wilful rebellion.

Pluto

Pluto reveals our ability to effect transformation. It shows where, and how, we experience regeneration.

The Aspects

When the planets positioned around the circle of the birth chart are a certain number of degrees apart, they are said to be in aspect. These aspects were once termed "benefic" or "malefic," but are now recognized as having harmonious, tense, or active qualities. The tense or active aspects are: square (90°), semisquare (45°), and opposition (180°). The harmonious aspects are: trine (120°), sextile (60°), and semisextile (30°).

Some Famous Birth Charts

H ere follow four famous birth charts—the position of the planets at the time of birth indicates the characteristics that led them to succeed in their chosen fields.

Tennis star
Libra and Gemini make a strong symbolic combination for a tennis player. Interesting that this Gemini plays great doubles with her sister.

Venus Williams
The winner of the ladies' championship at Wimbledon in 2000 has Sun Gemini, Moon Leo, and Mercury setting her in the public eye. Pluto in the first house on her Libran ascendant indicates her drive to succeed. Venus is close to the Sun in her chart, which shows her easy manner in interviews.

Margaret Thatcher
Britain's first female prime minister, known as the "Iron Lady," has magnetic Scorpio on her ascendant, while Saturn in Scorpio rising shows her almost ruthless determination to make her mark in life. The diplomatic Libran Sun has acquired a hard edge and here we see another Moon in Leo indicating her need to be in the public eye. However, Venus in Sagittarius in the first house shows that she has the ability to smile sweetly and get her own way when the arguments become intense.

Iron lady
Scorpio, her ascendant sign, is coruled by Mars. The corresponding metals of Mars are iron and steel, aptly expressing her iron will.

Superman

It is typical of Pluto closely conjuncting the ascendant, as in Christopher Reeve's chart, that this is a life of transforming destiny.

Christopher Reeve

A superman with a superman's chart, Reeve was a perfect choice for the comic-strip hero. When disaster suddenly struck in real life in the form of paralysis after a fall from a horse, his own heroism took over. Pluto in Leo on the ascendant, and trine Mars in the fifth house, indicate enormous power and bravery, and signify the archetypal reckless-hero type. Jupiter in the tenth house is square Pluto. This promises that he will never leave the public eye or be forgotten by his admirers, despite the transformation in his life.

Steven Spielberg

The brilliant filmmaker and storyteller has an adventurous Sagittarian Sun in the sixth house, making him far-seeking, but perfectionist, in his work. Opposite the Sun is the revolutionary, sometimes eccentric Uranus, which adds the theme of sudden, sharp shocks to his movies. The Moon, Jupiter, and Venus in Scorpio in the fifth house indicate creative passion. A Cancer ascendant shows great sensitivity and an emphasis on human (as well as extraterrestrial) relationships.

Storyteller

With Pisces on the midheaven (career), the ability to visualize and fantasize would have been an inevitable asset to the imaginative output of Steven Spielberg.

Dragon
A mythical beast, unlike the 11 other animals. Although frightening in Western mythology, the dragon has always been seen by the Chinese as a beneficent creature. It is thought that its origin may lie in the alligators of the Yangtze River.

CHINESE ASTROLOGY

China has a completely different system of astrology, which, although based on 12 signs, operates on a symbolic yearly change rather than the movement of celestial bodies. The legend says that Buddha invited the animals to celebrate the New Year with him, but only 12 arrived for the ceremony. As a reward, Buddha named a year after each of them. The years run in the order in which the animals arrived to meet the great Buddha: the Rat was the first to arrive and the Pig was the last. The natures of the 12 signs are well defined, and people born in the year of a particular animal are said to possess its qualities.

Moon cycle
Unlike the Western sun-sign system, the Chinese operate on the phases of the Moon's cycle and the lunar year. Each year, the New Year begins on a different date to that of the Western calendar, falling somewhere between January 21 and February 21.

The animal years

According to legend, Buddha invited all the animals
to a New Year celebration. Only 12 animals arrived at the
ceremony and they were rewarded by having a Chinese
astrological year named after each of them.

Chinese Year Tables

The Chinese calendar is a combination of lunar and solar movements. The lunar cycle is approximately 29.5 days. In order to "catch up" with the solar calendar, the Chinese add an extra month once every few years (every seven years out of a 19-year cycle). This is roughly the same as adding an extra day in leap years. This is why, when compared to our solar calendar, the Chinese New Year falls on a different date each year.

Chinese Year Chart

Year	From–To	Animal	Year	From–To	Animal
1912	Feb 18, 1912–Feb 5, 1913	Rat	1931	Feb 17, 1931–Feb 5, 1932	Sheep
1913	Feb 6, 1913–Jan 25, 1914	Ox	1932	Feb 6, 1932–Jan 25, 1933	Monkey
1914	Jan 26, 1914–Feb 13, 1915	Tiger	1933	Jan 26, 1933–Feb 13, 1934	Rooster
1915	Feb 14, 1915–Feb 2, 1916	Rabbit	1934	Feb 14, 1934–Feb 3, 1935	Dog
1916	Feb 3, 1916–Jan 22, 1917	Dragon	1935	Feb 4, 1935–Jan 23, 1936	Pig
1917	Jan 23, 1917–Feb 10, 1918	Snake	1936	Jan 24, 1936–Feb 10, 1937	Rat
1918	Feb 11, 1918–Jan 31, 1919	Horse	1937	Feb 11, 1937–Jan 30, 1938	Ox
1919	Feb 1, 1919–Feb 19, 1920	Sheep	1938	Jan 31, 1938–Feb 18, 1939	Tiger
1920	Feb 20, 1920–Feb 7, 1921	Monkey	1939	Feb 19, 1939–Feb 7, 1940	Rabbit
1921	Feb 8, 1921–Jan 27, 1922	Rooster	1940	Feb 8, 1940–Jan 26, 1941	Dragon
1922	Jan 28, 1922–Feb 15, 1923	Dog	1941	Jan 27, 1941–Feb 14, 1942	Snake
1923	Feb 16, 1923–Feb 4, 1924	Pig	1942	Feb 15, 1942–Feb 4, 1943	Horse
1924	Feb 5, 1924–Jan 24, 1925	Rat	1943	Feb 5, 1943–Jan 24, 1944	Sheep
1925	Jan 25, 1925–Feb 12, 1926	Ox	1944	Jan 25, 1944–Feb 12, 1945	Monkey
1926	Feb 13, 1926–Feb 1, 1927	Tiger	1945	Feb 13, 1945–Feb 1, 1946	Rooster
1927	Feb 2, 1927–Jan 22, 1928	Rabbit	1946	Feb 2, 1946–Jan 21, 1947	Dog
1928	Jan 23, 1928–Feb 9, 1929	Dragon	1947	Jan 22, 1947–Feb 9, 1948	Pig
1929	Feb 10, 1929–Jan 29, 1930	Snake	1948	Feb 10, 1948–Jan 28, 1949	Rat
1930	Jan 30, 1930–Feb 16, 1931	Horse	1949	Jan 29, 1949–Feb 16, 1950	Ox

Chinese Year Chart

Year	From–To	Animal	Year	From–To	Animal
1950	Feb 17, 1950–Feb 5, 1951	Tiger	**1981**	Feb 5, 1981–Jan 24, 1982	Rooster
1951	Feb 6, 1951–Jan 26, 1952	Rabbit	**1982**	Jan 25, 1982–Feb 12, 1983	Dog
1952	Jan 27, 1952–Feb 13, 1953	Dragon	**1983**	Feb 13, 1983–Feb 1, 1984	Pig
1953	Feb 14, 1953–Feb 2, 1954	Snake	**1984**	Feb 2, 1984–Feb 19, 1985	Rat
1954	Feb 3, 1954–Jan 23, 1955	Horse	**1985**	Feb 20, 1985–Feb 8, 1986	Ox
1955	Jan 24, 1955–Feb 11, 1956	Sheep	**1986**	Feb 9, 1986–Jan 28, 1987	Tiger
1956	Feb 12, 1956–Jan 30, 1957	Monkey	**1987**	Jan 29, 1987–Feb 16, 1988	Rabbit
1957	Jan 31, 1957–Feb 17, 1958	Rooster	**1988**	Feb 17, 1988–Feb 5, 1989	Dragon
1958	Feb 18, 1958–Feb 7, 1959	Dog	**1989**	Feb 6, 1989–Jan 26, 1990	Snake
1959	Feb 8, 1959–Jan 27, 1960	Pig	**1990**	Jan 27, 1990–Feb 14, 1991	Horse
1960	Jan 28, 1960–Feb 14, 1961	Rat	**1991**	Feb 15, 1991–Feb 3, 1992	Sheep
1961	Feb 15, 1961–Feb 4, 1962	Ox	**1992**	Feb 4, 1992–Jan 22, 1993	Monkey
1962	Feb 5, 1962–Jan 24, 1963	Tiger	**1993**	Jan 23, 1993–Feb 9, 1994	Rooster
1963	Jan 25, 1963–Feb 12, 1964	Rabbit	**1994**	Feb 10, 1994–Jan 30, 1995	Dog
1964	Feb 13, 1964–Feb 1, 1965	Dragon	**1995**	Jan 31, 1995–Feb 18, 1996	Pig
1965	Feb 2, 1965–Jan 20, 1966	Snake	**1996**	Feb 19, 1996–Feb 6, 1997	Rat
1966	Jan 21, 1966–Feb 8, 1967	Horse	**1997**	Feb 7, 1997–Jan 27, 1998	Ox
1967	Feb 9, 1967–Jan 29, 1968	Sheep	**1998**	Jan 28, 1998–Feb 15, 1999	Tiger
1968	Jan 30, 1968–Feb 16, 1969	Monkey	**1999**	Feb 16, 1999–Feb 4, 2000	Rabbit
1969	Feb 17, 1969–Feb 5, 1970	Rooster	**2000**	Feb 5, 2000–Jan 23, 2001	Dragon
1970	Feb 6, 1970–Jan 26, 1971	Dog	**2001**	Jan 24, 2001–Feb 11, 2002	Snake
1971	Jan 27, 1971–Feb 15, 1972	Pig	**2002**	Feb 12, 2002–Jan 31, 2003	Horse
1972	Feb 16, 1972–Feb 2, 1973	Rat	**2003**	Feb 1, 2003–Jan 21, 2004	Sheep
1973	Feb 3, 1973–Jan 22, 1974	Ox	**2004**	Jan 22, 2004–Feb 8, 2005	Monkey
1974	Jan 23, 1974–Feb 10, 1975	Tiger	**2005**	Feb 9, 2005–Jan 28, 2006	Rooster
1975	Feb 11, 1975–Jan 30, 1976	Rabbit	**2006**	Jan 29, 2006–Feb 17, 2007	Dog
1976	Jan 31, 1976–Feb 17, 1977	Dragon	**2007**	Feb 18, 2007–Feb 6, 2008	Pig
1977	Feb 18, 1977–Feb 6, 1978	Snake	**2008**	Feb 7, 2008–Jan 25, 2009	Rat
1978	Feb 7, 1978–Jan 27, 1979	Horse	**2009**	Jan 26, 2009–Feb 13, 2010	Ox
1979	Jan 28, 1979–Feb 15, 1980	Sheep	**2010**	Feb 14, 2010–Feb 2, 2011	Tiger
1980	Feb 16, 1980–Feb 4, 1981	Monkey	**2011**	Feb 3, 2011–Jan 22, 2012	Rabbit

The Ox
One of the most domesticated animals in the Chinese zodiac, the ox is a sign of good fortune through necessary hard work.

THE FIRST SIX ANIMAL SIGNS

The first six animals to visit Buddha on New Year's Day were the Rat, Ox, Tiger, Rabbit, Dragon, and Snake. Chinese astrology comprises much more than just the 12 animals. These define the 12 basic types of personality, but further nuances are provided by someone's year, month, day, and hour of birth.

Rat	Ox	Tiger

Rat

Forthright, honest, and blessed with more than a fair share of charm, Rat people are hard-working and thrifty. Bright, happy, and sociable, but not always as generous as other animal signs, Rat people prefer exclusivity and have a close circle of friends.

Compatible with Dragon, Ox, and Monkey.

Incompatible with Rabbit and Horse.

Ox

Those born in the year of the Ox get on in life through their own hard work. They are dependable and calm, preferring routine and conventional behavior. Because of their trustworthy character, they achieve positions of authority and responsibility.

Compatible with Rooster, Rat, and Snake.

Incompatible with Monkey, Sheep, and Tiger.

Tiger

Magnetic and respected leader types, Tiger people are rash and rebellious. Capable of both generous gestures and petty meanness, they have a vigorous love of life that is stimulating, although their love of action can lead them into impetuous behavior.

Compatible with Horse, Dragon, and Dog.

Incompatible with Snake, Monkey, Ox, and Rabbit.

Astrological wheel

A Nepalese thangka depicting the zodiacal oracle with the 12 Chinese astrological animals arranged around the edge. Buddhist symbols decorate the inner wheel. At the root of Chinese astrology are the yearly cycles of the animals.

<table>
<tr><td>

Rabbit

</td><td>

Dragon

</td><td>

Snake

</td></tr>
<tr><td>

Those born in the year of the Rabbit make warm and affectionate friends. They are clever, peace-loving, contented, and they enjoy showing off their talents. The Rabbit is said to be one of the most fortunate of the 12 signs and is ruled by the Moon.

Compatible with Sheep, Dog, and Pig.

Incompatible with Rat, Tiger, and Rooster.

</td><td>

There is a magical quality about natives of this sign. They are magnanimous, full of vitality, and love color and movement. They need a mission in life in order to give of their best, and to find a Dragon without a cause is rare.

Compatible with Rat, Snake, Rooster, and Monkey.

Incompatible with Dog and Ox.

</td><td>

The deepest thinkers of the Chinese zodiac, Snake people make good philosophers, politicians, and financiers. Usually elegant, attractive, and self-critical, and also good-natured snobs, they are often lucky with money and tend to exaggerate.

Compatible with Rooster, Ox, Dragon, and Dog.

Incompatible with Tiger and Pig.

</td></tr>
</table>

The Year's Influence
—The First Six Signs

From rat to snake these years favor success and financial gain. Years of drama are followed by periods of peace and reflection.

Year of the Rat

This year of plenty is auspicious for acquiring wealth and making long-term investments, but it is not wise to take unnecessary risks. It favors Rats, Oxen, Dragons, Monkeys, and Pigs, but is a bad year for Tigers, Rabbits, Horses, Sheep, and Roosters, and an indifferent one for Snakes and Dogs.

Year of the Ox

A year of responsibility, conscientious effort, and the settling of domestic affairs. Gain is possible, but only from devoted, persistent hard work. It favors Oxen, Horses, Monkeys, and Roosters, but is bad for Tigers, Snakes, Sheep, and Dogs, and indifferent to Rats, Rabbits, Dragons, and Pigs.

Year of the Tiger

This is an explosive and aggressive year. More positively, however, things done on a large scale can expect success. It is a time of great extremes, when fortunes are made and lost and people are impelled to behave overdramatically. Although it favors Tigers, Dragons, Horses, and Dogs, it is a bad year for Oxen, Rats, Roosters, and Sheep, and an indifferent one for Rabbits, Snakes, Pigs, and Monkeys.

Year of the Rabbit

Diplomacy wins over aggression in this relaxed, congenial year. Lifestyles can become more leisurely and easy-going, but care should be taken not to overindulge. Making money is easier in a Rabbit year. It favors Rabbits, Dragons, Snakes, Horses, Sheep, and Monkeys, but is bad for Rats, and indifferent to Oxen, Tigers, Roosters, Dogs, and Pigs.

Year of the Dragon

A year for big schemes and projects, although it would be wise not to overestimate one's abilities. However, it is a good time for making money in easy ways and is traditionally considered an auspicious year for getting married. Although it favors Rats, Tigers, Dragons, Monkeys, and Roosters, it is a bad year for Dogs, and an indifferent one for Oxen, Rabbits, Snakes, Pigs, Horses, and Sheep.

Year of the Snake

This is a year for shrewdness, common sense, and reflection. A good time for commerce, although thought should be given to the negotiation of business deals. Arts, sophistication, and fashion are highlighted. Although it favors Rabbits, Dragons, Snakes, Sheep, Monkeys, and Dogs, it is a bad year for Rats, Oxen, and Tigers, and an indifferent one for Roosters, Horses, and Pigs.

The Monkey

Imaginative, versatile, and always on the move, the Monkey has a lot in common with the qualities of Gemini in Western astrology.

THE LAST SIX ANIMAL SIGNS

Understanding the differences in temperament between yourself and others will help you to accept and deal comfortably with people instead of getting irritated with them. You can also choose particular animal signs to mediate for you in a dispute.

Horse	Sheep	Monkey

Horse

At their very best when they are the center of attention, when the world focuses on them, Horse people can achieve unlimited success. Quick-witted, attractive, and healthy, they love crowds and flattery. They may indulge in explosive outbursts, but soon forget their anger.

Compatible with Goat, Dog, Tiger, and Rooster.

Incompatible with Rat, Monkey, Ox, and Pig.

Sheep

The most feminine sign, the Sheep is a creative hedonist, often with great artistic talent, ruled by emotions. They may be pessimistic and insecure, while their sympathetic nature is easily taken in by sob stories. Their outer gentleness belies strong determination and perseverance.

Compatible with Horse, Pig, Rabbit, and Monkey.

Incompatible with Ox and Dog.

Monkey

Bright, friendly, and unscrupulous opportunists, those born in this year are initially enthusiastic, but easily tire of projects. Usually versatile in the extreme, they are able to solve the most intricate problems if they don't lose interest in them.

Compatible with Dragon, Rat, and Sheep.

Incompatible with Tiger, Horse, and Pig.

The Sheep

It is rare for the natives of a Sheep year not to have some artistic talent. Andy Warhol and Michelangelo were artists who shared this sign.

Rooster	Dog	Pig

Roosters appear self-assured and eccentric, but can actually be quite conservative and old-fashioned. Extravagant in their gestures, they sometimes take on too much, but often succeed beyond all expectations.

Compatible with Ox, Snake, Horse, Dragon, Dog, and Rat.

Incompatible with Rabbit and other Roosters.

Dog people are honest, faithful, respect tradition, value honor, enjoy helping others, and are the first to speak out against injustice. Not interested in socializing, they rarely shine in company, but are caring, intelligent, and good listeners.

Compatible with Horse, Tiger, and Rabbit.

Incompatible with Dragon and Sheep.

Quiet Pig people study a lot because they want to gain knowledge. Although they don't make many friends, they keep those they do make because they're honest, kind, and true to others, and are models of sincerity, purity, tolerance, and honor.

Compatible with Rabbit, Dragon, and Sheep.

Incompatible with Snake and Monkey.

The Year's Influence —The Last Six Signs

From Horse to Pig, these years promise excitement and action between periods of calm and domestic harmony.

Year of the Horse

A lively, hectic, somewhat frustrating year, its keyword is action, although there will be some frustration. It is time to follow intuition and take risks. It favors Oxen, Dragons, Sheep, and Roosters, is bad for Horses, Rats, Snakes, and Pigs, and indifferent for Tigers, Rabbits, Monkeys, and Dogs.

Year of the Sheep

In contrast, this is a calm, smooth-running year. It is a good time to travel and make new friends. Imaginative ventures will succeed. Good for Sheep, Monkeys, and Pigs, it is a bad year for Oxen, Tigers, Roosters, and Dogs, and indifferent for Rats, Rabbits, Dragons, Snakes, and Horses.

Year of the Monkey

The Monkey's year usually involves much wheeler-dealing and negotiation. The temptation to gamble and speculate can either reap huge dividends or result in great setbacks. Although it favors Rats, Tigers, Horses, Sheep, Dogs, Pigs, Monkeys, and Roosters, it is a bad year for Oxen, and an indifferent one for Rabbits, Dragons, and Snakes.

Year of the Rooster

Another optimistic year, but this one can go over the top. In the end one may discover it has been a time when one has to expend the maximum effort for the minimum gain. Also a year when one may become too self-obsessed to hear what others are saying. Although this year favors Rats, Dragons, Horses, Roosters, and Pigs, it is a bad year for Tigers, Rabbits, and Snakes, and an indifferent one for Oxen, Sheep, Dogs, and Monkeys.

Year of the Dog

Usually a year of domestic happiness and harmony, this is the perfect time to reassess that which we value. Although a generally calm period, there may be brief clashes where good causes are concerned. Although it favors Rats, Dragons, Dogs, and Pigs, it is a bad year for Oxen, Snakes, Sheep, and Roosters, and an indifferent one for Tigers, Rabbits, Horses, and Monkeys.

Year of the Pig

A year of goodwill and plenty. This is, however, the kind of year in which we must beware of being seduced into overspending and making ill-advised investments. It is a great deal easier to make friends at this time. Although it favors Rats, Tigers, Rabbits, Dragons, Horses, Monkeys, and Pigs, it is a bad year for nobody, and an indifferent one for Oxen, Snakes, Sheep, Roosters, and Dogs.

DOWSING

Dowsing has been in existence for so long that it is extraordinary that there are not more references to the skill in early literature. ❧ It is recorded in an old Arabic manuscript that, when the Queen of Sheba visited Solomon, she had dowsers among her train who divined for gold and water. Even more ancient cave paintings in the Sahara, dating from around 6000 BC, show a person holding what is believed to be a divining rod. ❧ Myths and legends tell of magical rods used by Hermes and Aaron, although it is difficult to define when dowsing rods and magic wands became separate. Greek and Roman literature also make reference to rhabdomancy, the system of divining with rods, arrows, or wands.

The Dowser's Art

The pendulum
The most portable of all dowsing tools, the pendulum can be incorporated into personal jewelry in the form of crystals and other gems.

The earliest mention of dowsing in England was made in fifteenth-century records that state that German dowsers were imported into Cornwall to find lost tin mines. Local inhabitants thus learned the art of dowsing, and for that reason western England became more famous for its inhabitants' dowsing abilities than other parts of the country.

The subjects of ivory engravings on Saxon mining tools dating from between 1664 and 1749 are figures of men using divining rods and pendulums. It was thought that hazel twigs, or *baguettes divinatoires* (the French for "divinatory sticks"), were more effective if they were cut when the heavens were propitious, and astrological charts were therefore cast to discover the most appropriate time.

Although there are a vast number of dowsing instruments, they mainly fall into four categories: the forked twig, the spring rod, the twin-angle rods, and the pendulum. Learning to use a divination tool, like learning a musical instrument, is purely a matter of practice. It is a skill that anyone can learn, but some people are better at it than others. After experimentation, one method will often prove to be more suited to a person's sensitivity than another.

Dowsing, which is traditionally associated with the search for water and minerals below ground, has acquired a greater respectability than other means of divination; perhaps the fact that farmers and surveyors are often connected with the work of dowsers attaches validity to the technique.

How does it work?

Although many proposals have been made to explain how dowsing works—ranging from the diviner's response, to the electromagnetic fields of objects and paranormal phenomena—no one knows. Arguments that there is a scientific basis for dowsing, with the possibility of direct electrical emanations from underground sources being picked up by the dowser's own complex metabolism, fall away when one considers map dowsing, however. A good dowser can find water, iron, utility pipes, electric cables, lost objects, and buried treasure by working a pendulum over maps and plans of buildings.

Even police forces have sought the assistance of dowsers to obtain information in crime detection.

Dowsing Instruments

Most of the instruments used in dowsing amplify the minute human neuromuscular responses generated when dowsing, which tell you what your hands are doing.

Wire rods

The metal to make your rods can very often be found in stores selling model-making supplies. Welding rods are a good alternative.

DOWSING WITH RODS
The most familiar use for dowsing rods is in water divining. There is no particular reason why this is so, because it is possible to dowse almost anything once one is adept at using the rods or pendulum. It is good, however, to start with water, because it is the underground substance that we are most likely to find easily. Do not give up if you do not seem to be having great success initially: the more you practice, the more sensitive and less self-conscious you will become. As with the pendulum, divining rods must become an extension of your own sensitivity to the world around you, and this takes time.

Making dowsing rods

You will need two metal rods, each about 20 inches (50 centimeters) in length. The most popular are welding rods that are sufficiently thin to bend easily. You will need to bend the rods to obtain two rods with a handle (which should be as identical as possible), so that there is a 90° angle between the handle and the rest of the rod. The handles should be around 4–5 inches (10–12 centimeters) long.

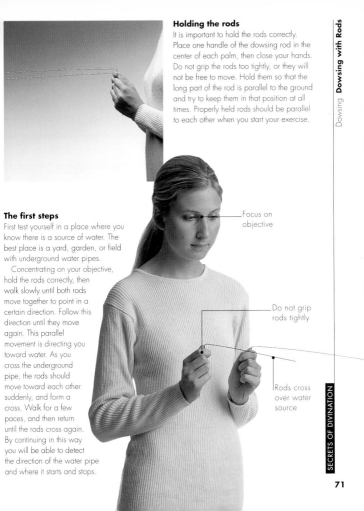

Holding the rods

It is important to hold the rods correctly. Place one handle of the dowsing rod in the center of each palm, then close your hands. Do not grip the rods too tightly, or they will not be free to move. Hold them so that the long part of the rod is parallel to the ground and try to keep them in that position at all times. Properly held rods should be parallel to each other when you start your exercise.

The first steps

First test yourself in a place where you know there is a source of water. The best place is a yard, garden, or field with underground water pipes.

Concentrating on your objective, hold the rods correctly, then walk slowly until both rods move together to point in a certain direction. Follow this direction until they move again. This parallel movement is directing you toward water. As you cross the underground pipe, the rods should move toward each other suddenly, and form a cross. Walk for a few paces, and then return until the rods cross again. By continuing in this way you will be able to detect the direction of the water pipe and where it starts and stops.

Focus on objective

Do not grip rods tightly

Rods cross over water source

Types of Dowsing

The map

It is best to make photocopies of the map areas you wish to dowse. This enables you to color your own grid lines.

Dowsing has been successfully used to locate fish in lakes, archaeological sites and artifacts, unmarked graves, lost objects or valuables, and so forth. In criminal cases, dowsing has been used to find murder weapons, to determine whether a person is dead or alive merely by using their photograph, to locate missing persons, and even to discover whether letters, wills, and signatures are genuine or forged.

Field dowsing

Field dowsing is the traditional use of dowsing that involves locating water, objects, and so forth, on a given terrain. This technique is also known as "witching the area."

The use of samples is important when one is looking for a specific material or object. If, for example, one is using dowsing rods instead of a metal detector to look for old artifacts, when walking over a field one would loosely hold an old coin or small piece of silver against one of the handles of the rod. This type of "affinity" dowsing is common. It appears that the material in the hand makes a psychic connection with similar hidden materials. Many dowsers have made surprising archaeological finds in this manner, discovering old battlegrounds and settlements. It is possible that powerful periods in history maintain a kind of etheric resonance long after their physical evidence has been swallowed up by time and has been covered by the countryside.

Remote dowsing

Witching the area is not used in this approach. Instead, the dowser locates the target or information from any distance by the following means.

Map dowsing: the dowser locates the target using a map or sketch, which, because of the scale, is better suited to the use of a pendulum. There are no distance limits here, since the dowser can locate his or her target from thousands of miles (or kilometers) away.

Information dowsing: the dowser obtains the necessary information on any subject without space or time limits. This is done in the form of questions and answers, dowsing over words and numbers on boards, photographs, and personal articles belonging to the person being inquired about.

Undiscovered Energy

Some scientists have begun to take dowsing more seriously in recent years because good dowsers tend to have a very high success rate at locating what they seek. They think dowsers may tap into an undiscovered form of energy.

Improvise

If you are caught without a pendulum, almost anything of a suitable weight and size can be utilized. The most common is a wedding ring tied to a hair.

THE PENDULUM

Almost any small object attached to a thin thread or cord can be used as a pendulum. The most important requirement, however, is that the object should be symmetrical: a pendulum with a wobble is not conducive to sympathetic dowsing. Although commercial pendula (or "bobs," as they are also known) are made from practically any material that can be shaped, such as metal, plastic, wood, and crystal, the final choice as to which is best will be a matter of personal preference.

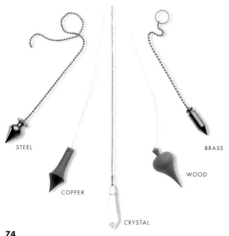

STEEL

COPPER

CRYSTAL

WOOD

BRASS

The pendula

There is a wide variety of pendula and threads to choose from. Some people prefer wooden bobs, since they feel metals give a bias to intrusive vibrations from other metal objects around. The best thing is to experiment with different materials and use what feels most comfortable for you.

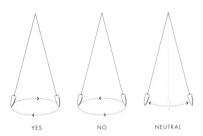

YES NO NEUTRAL

Three basic answers

There are three basic answers that a pendulum can give you: "Yes," "No," and "Neutral" (the latter may mean "don't know," "unsure," and so on—you must decide). Then decide which direction signifies each answer. In this illustration "Yes" is a clockwise motion, "No" is counterclockwise, and "Neutral" is either motionless or a back-and-forth movement.

The dowse

There is obviously a thin dividing line between no conscious movement of the hand at all and a slight initiatory action to set the pendulum in motion. If the hand is so rigidly held to cause the pendulum to remain motionless, you are not in a receptive and sensitive mood for making a dowse.

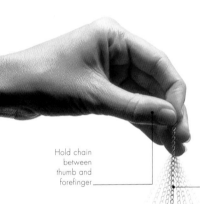

Hold chain between thumb and forefinger

Hold more than 3–4 inches (8–10 centimeters) above pendulum

Teaching Your Pendulum

The glass of water test

This test has similarities to the street gambler's three-card "find-the-lady" trick. You're a top dowser when you can detect a winner every time.

All questions should be framed to accommodate the simple triad of answers: "Yes," "No," and "Neutral." You would not ask, "Where are my lost keys?" for instance. This would be impossible for the pendulum to answer. You would rephrase the question to ask, "Are the lost keys in the house?" If the answer is "Yes," the next question would be "Are they upstairs?" and so on, until the location is discovered. Although it is you who is learning the art of dowsing, you must

treat your pendulum as a creature that needs to be trained in your ways and system of understanding. The simplest technique is as follows.

If you decide that a clockwise gyration means "Yes," counterclockwise means "No," and back and forth in a straight line or no movement at all means "Neutral," you would proceed to teach the pendulum as follows.

Hold the string between your thumb and forefinger, no more than about 3–4 inches (8–10 centimeters) above the pendulum, with your elbow resting comfortably on a table, and concentrate on the word "Yes" while imagining a clockwise movement of the bob. Try not to set it in motion by any involuntary movement; just use the power of your mind. When you have achieved this, stop the movement and repeat the process again and again, until you are totally unaware that it is you who is making the pendulum move.

Now repeat the process while thinking the word "No" and producing a counterclockwise gyration. Repeat the process as before until you feel at one with the word and the movement.

Finally, experiment with the word "Neutral," visualizing the pendulum moving back and forth in a straight line.

The salt water test

Once you are confident that the pendulum seems to show a life of its own, you have passed the first test. Now for the moment of truth: your abilities are testable, and you will need the help of a sympathetic and patient friend for this. The simplest way to try out your new abilities is the saltwater test.

Prepare three small glasses of water, one of which should contain a well-dissolved teaspoon of salt. Look away as your partner rearranges the glasses, then relax, and slowly dowse each one to discover which contains the salty water. (Any dispute can be solved with a sip.) Although you won't necessarily get it right every time, you will eventually reach a stage when you are picking the correct glass more than a third of the time.

The location

If you have photographs of the area you are dowsing, study and absorb these images before making your pendulum pass over the map.

MAP DOWSING
When you're using a map, remember that it is purely a reference on which to focus questions, and not an object in its own right. In other words, you aren't really dowsing the map itself, so there is no need to orient the map north, south, and so on. When working on the map, imagine yourself walking around the area that it defines. Get an overall feeling for this area, build up your sensitivity to it, and remain conscious of and focused on the subject of your search.

The area method

When locating things with this method, you will need to have some kind of grid on the map. Some maps may already have one, on other maps, mark an even grid in pencil. Depending on the search, start with large squares—say about 3 miles (5 kilometers) square—and run through them in sequence, asking "Is the object in this square?" for each of the squares in turn. Once the pendulum reacts positively to a square, break down that square into smaller squares—perhaps 1 mile (or 1 kilometer) square—and repeat the process. Continue for as long as is necessary and practical, using smaller and smaller squares, until you find the exact position of the object.

The coordinates method

When using the coordinates method, instead of using squares as described in the area method, select a row on, say, the north–south axis of the map and ask "Is it on this line?" continuing along this axis until you receive a positive response. Now do the same on the east–west axis to find the appropriate row. The point on the map given by these two coordinates—the map reference—should give the location of the object.

The tracking method

Tracking on a map can only be done with a pendulum. Using the area or coordinates methods, once the pendulum is closing in on the location, a pointer or pencil point can be used in the final square to move along and around it. Observe closely the minute differences in the pendulum's movements. The positional techniques used in map dowsing are similar to those used for on-site work: the area, or grid, method; the coordinates, or triangulation, method; and the tracking method.

Use the pendulum to dowse for a more exact location

Pencil marks the spot

The Y-Rod and the Bobber

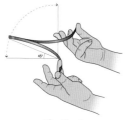

The Y-rod

The Y-rod can be made of wood, metal, or plastic. Dowsers in the early 1900s used flexible whalebone strips.

The final two dowsing methods are no less popular than those previously outlined, but still have their advantages and disadvantages. They are worth trying before you settle on your perfect tool.

The Y-rod

The Y-rod is the traditional forked stick or hazel twig. It can be made of wood, metal, or plastic. The material most popularly used nowadays is plastic. A Y-rod can easily be made from two slim, springy, plastic strips bound together at one end. The best length is usually around 16–20 inches (40–50 centimeters).

Hold the Y-rod with the joined end pointing downward. Your thumbs should face upward and your palms toward the center. Hold the rods tightly and spread the "Y" outward by rotating your wrist outward. Your thumbs should now be pointing outward and your palms should be facing upward. The Y-rod will flip, and will usually point upward at an angle of about 45° to indicate the ready position.

Swinging down from the ready position is normally the "Yes" response and an indicator of water or whatever other material is being sought. Swinging up from the ready position normally signifies "No."

Y-rods are very responsive and act quickly. They work well when the diviner is walking over uneven ground and are reliable in fairly rough, windy weather. They are not, however, as versatile as other methods because they only have an up-and-down motion. You will, therefore, need to move your body in order to locate a specific direction.

The bobber

The bobber is made from any flexible rod, branch, or wire and measures between 16 and 36 inches (40 and 90 centimeters) in length. It usually has a coiled wire and a weighted tip.

Bobbers must be suspended pointing downward at a 45° angle. You can program them to copy the pendulum by bobbing up and down for "Yes," moving sideways for "No," and staying at the 45° angle for a neutral decision. Alternatively, you can program them to respond in any way you like, perhaps by swinging back and forth toward a target and by spinning when above the target. They can replace the pendulum for most field work but can be a little delicate and awkward to carry.

CARTOMANCY

The origin of telling fortunes with playing cards has a dim and distant past and is associated far more than the tarot with family fortune-telling. There was always an aged aunt or a knowing granny who could "read" the cards. There would often be wild claims that she was the seventh child of a seventh child and just "knew" things. ⮞ On an auspicious day, and with much ceremony, the worn deck was taken from its painted tin box, which was kept on the mantelpiece, and the family fortunes would be told.

Suits and Symbols

The variety of different designs and symbols that have led to the simple playing cards that we know today is infinite. They are now great collector's items, and the search for them can be a lifetime's hobby.

The original cards seem to have evolved around 1320, and have spread in profusion across the world since then. Some of the differences between the decks of other countries indicate the various stages in the evolution of the present decks. The French always name their court cards, for example, while Spanish card suits are cups, swords, clubs, and coins. German decks introduced hearts, bells, leaves, and acorns.

The interpretation of each card was basic and simple, unlike the deep, esoteric meanings of the tarot. There is a fatalistic approach to most of the

Hearts

This suit represents emotional matters, love, friendship, and marriage. Hearts also signify joy, liberality, and good temper. With few of these in a reading, one can consider the question to be ruled by logic rather than feelings, and an unemotional decision can be made.

Diamonds

This suit represents money and possessions in the broadest sense. With many diamonds showing in a reading, the indication is that financial or material considerations are of the greatest importance to the question. They can also denote delay, quarrels, and annoyance.

cards' meanings, perhaps because they developed in a much earlier time, when life was more eventful and hazardous.

Each suit has certain symbolic connotations, primarily related to the practical and emotional aspects of life. The concerns of human beings recur in every divinatory process—even the humble playing card has not escaped our attempt to attach symbolic significance to it.

Clubs	Spades
This suit denotes work and business interests, ambition, and career matters. A large number of clubs indicates that a path to success can be found. Clubs promise happiness, and, no matter how many negative cards there are, they rarely signify bad fortune.	This suit indicates hopes and expectations, but also disappointment and frustration. If a reading shows a great many of these cards, it is an indication of adverse influences at work. They can also signify grief, sickness, and loss of money.

Queen of hearts
The late Princess Diana famously declared that she wanted to be the "queen of hearts," referring to her love of people, rather than a love of power.

COURT·CARDS As in all card games, among the court

cards the ace ranks the highest in value and importance. Then comes the king, followed by the queen, the knave, ten, nine, eight, and seven, with the other numbers following in their decreasing order. In many cases, the position of the cards can change their signification entirely, their individual and relative meanings often being widely different.

Hearts

Ace of Hearts
The house, home, and family.

King of Hearts
A fair man, of good-natured disposition, but impetuous.

Queen of Hearts
A fair woman, faithful, prudent, and affectionate.

Knave of Hearts
The dearest friend, male or female, of the questioner.

Diamonds

Ace of Diamonds
Important letter—neighboring cards reveal the content.

King of Diamonds
A fair man, hot-tempered, obstinate, and vengeful.

Queen of Diamonds
A fair woman, fond of company, and a flirt.

Knave of Diamonds
A self-obsessed relation.

Clubs

Ace of Clubs
Wealth, happiness, and peace of mind.

Ace of Clubs
A dark man, upright, faithful, and affectionate.

Ace of Clubs
A dark woman, gentle and pleasing.

Ace of Clubs
A sincere, but impetuous, friend.

Spades

Ace of Spades
Misfortune, spiteful intentions.

King of Spades
A dark, ambitious man.

Queen of Spades
A malicious, dark woman, generally a widow.

Knave of Spades
An indolent, envious person.

Numbered Cards

Numbered cards
Although most numbered cards just show the requisite number of suit symbols, some decks are beautifully decorated with elaborate illustrations.

The numbered cards all have individual meanings, which vary in the different suits. Each meaning must be considered according to the areas with which each suit is concerned.

Hearts

Ten of Hearts Happiness and many children. This card alters positively any adjacent bad cards and improves any good ones.

Nine of Hearts Wealth and high esteem; also the wish card.

Eight of Hearts Great pleasure and good company.

Seven of Hearts A fickle and false friend; be on your guard.

Six of Hearts A generous, but credulous, person.

Five of Hearts Troubles caused by unfounded jealousy.

Four of Hearts A person indifferent to the questioner's friendship.

Three of Hearts Trouble caused by the questioner's own imprudence.

Two of Hearts Great success, but much care and attention is needed in order to secure this.

Diamonds

Ten of Diamonds Money.

Nine of Diamonds Much travel is indicated in the near future.

Eight of Diamonds Shows a marriage late in life.

Seven of Diamonds Scandal and malicious gossip.

Six of Diamonds An early marriage that does not last.

Five of Diamonds Some unexpected news is indicated.

Four of Diamonds Trouble that arises

because of unfaithful friends; also a betrayed secret.

Three of Diamonds Quarrels, lawsuits, and domestic disagreements.

Two of Diamonds An engagement that is made or maintained against the wishes of friends.

Clubs

Ten of Clubs Unexpected riches; also the loss of a friend's company.

Nine of Clubs Acting against a friend's advice.

Eight of Clubs A covetous or greedy man; this card also warns against indulging in speculation.

Seven of Clubs Good fortune and happiness, but this card warns against the opposite sex.

Six of Clubs A lucrative business.

Five of Clubs A good marriage.

Four of Clubs Indecision; a change of objective for the sake of money.

Three of Clubs Shows more than one marriage.

Two of Clubs A disappointment is indicated.

Spades

Ten of Spades Bad luck and worry, particularly regarding financial affairs.

Nine of Spades Indicates bad luck in most things.

Eight of Spades A warning to be cautious in one's undertakings.

Seven of Spades Loss of an acquaintance, with attendant complications.

Six of Spades Some financial improvement through hard work—perhaps a raise in wages or a promotion at one's place of work.

Five of Spades A bad temper that requires correcting.

Four of Spades Some opposition and anxiety, but eventual improvement, in the workplace and elsewhere.

Three of Spades An eventful journey, possibly one that is related to your occupation.

Two of Spades A period of separation, scandal, and adverse gossip.

Your deck
As with tarot, it is good to keep at least two decks, one used for readings for others and one for personal readings. The latter should not be touched by any other person.

HOW TO DO A READING Although any

playing cards can be used in a reading, it will add a great deal of extra magic to the operation if you can acquire an old or unusual deck of cards. It is worth searching antique fairs, flea markets, and similar sources for that "special" deck that will give you enormous pleasure to use. They needn't cost a fortune, but it is worth buying cards that "speak" to you. Keep them somewhere special, too, and wrap them in a silk cloth. You'll build a rapport with them that makes them old friends.

Telling Whether You Will Get Your Wish

For a simple answer to a simple question, shuffle the cards well, all the while keeping your thoughts fixed upon whatever wish you may have formed. Cut them once, note which card you cut, and then return it to the deck. This card will have a bearing on the question.

Shuffle the cards again and deal them into three piles. Examine each of the piles in turn. If you find the card that you found when you first cut the deck in the same pile as a court card that most represents yourself, along with the Ace of Hearts or the Nine of Hearts, you will get your wish. However, if the Nine of Spades makes an appearance in the pile, it negates the other cards and you may count on disappointment.

The reading

After having shuffled the cards well, cut them three times, then lay them in three rows of three cards each, as shown opposite.

• The top row represents the past, with the central card giving the main meaning and the two on either side having a bearing on, and modifying, the meaning of the main card.

• The next row represents the present, with the central card stating the main situation and the two cards on either side developing the theme.

• The bottom row shows the future, with the central card again showing the main issue and the other cards modifying and accenting it.

Past

Ten of Spades (Bad luck and worry)

Two of Hearts (Success, care of details)

Ten of Diamonds (Money)

The central card shows that a possible contract offer has been made. The left-hand card says that there has been some bad luck and probably some money worries. The right-hand card indicates good money prospects.

Present

King of Clubs (Faithful man)

Knave of Spades (Envious person, rival)

Three of Diamonds (Quarrels, law suits)

The central card suggests that someone is contriving against the questioner—a competitor, perhaps? The left-hand card is a helpful friend, and the right-hand card warns of legal matters or quarrels.

Future

Two of Diamonds (Against advice)

Eight of spades (Cautious undertaking)

Two of Clubs (Disappointment)

The central card is a warning. The left-hand card indicates going against a friend's advice, which may refer to the King of Clubs friend in the second row, while the right-hand card indicates disappointment.

PAST

PRESENT

FUTURE

Summing Up

The questioner needs the money and a job offer looks good. Someone doesn't want her to get the job, however, and a friend advises her against making the move. If she takes the job, she should read the small print carefully and be prepared for disappointment if she goes against her friend's advice.

The Significance of Same-Numbered Cards

Jack
The terms Jack and Knave both originated as words for "child," but later became synonymous with servant.

Two Aces An intrigue; if a card is reversed, it will not succeed.

Four Kings A consultation on important business, the result of which will be highly satisfactory; if reversed, success will be doubtful.

Three Kings Important visitors with the ability to assist the questioner.

Two Kings A partnership in business; if reversed, its dissolution sometimes denotes friendly projects only.

Four Queens Company or society; one or more reversed denotes that the entertainment will be marred.

Three Queens Friendly calls; if any are reversed, gossip, scandal, or deceit.

Two Queens A meeting between friends; if either is reversed, trouble between friends.

Four Knaves A noisy party of mainly young people; if a card is reversed, a drinking bout.

Commit the following meanings to memory, but remember that they are like the alphabet of a printed book. With a little practice, you will soon be able to form these mystical letters into words, and the words into phrases that interpret the reading.

Four Aces Danger, failure in business, and legal problems; if one or more is reversed, the danger becomes less.

Three Aces Good tidings; if a card is reversed, folly.

Three Knaves False friends; if one or more is reversed, a quarrel with an ignorant person.

Two Knaves Evil intentions; if either is reversed, danger.

Four Tens Great success in a projected enterprise; if any are reversed, the success will be less brilliant.

Three Tens Improper conduct; if any are reversed, a failure.

Two Tens A change of trade or profession; if either is reversed, the possibility is distant.

Four Nines A great surprise; if any are reversed, an important public dinner.

Three Nines Joy, fortune, and health; reversed, wealth lost by bad judgement.

Marking Reversed Cards

Note that in order to know whether the Ace, Ten, Nine, Eight, and Seven of Diamonds are reversed, it helps to make a small pencil mark on each to show which is the top of the card.

Two Nines A little gain; if reversed, trifling losses when gambling.

Four Eights A short journey; if a card is reversed, the return of a friend or relative.

Three Eights Thoughts of marriage; if reversed, an affair or flirtation.

Two Eights A brief affair; if a card is reversed, small pleasures and brief adventures.

Four Sevens Intrigues, tricks, and disputes; reversed, they will rebound on the perpetrators.

Three Sevens Sickness; if reversed, a slight and brief indisposition.

Two Sevens Great amusement; if reversed, some regrets.

When card reading developed, the gypsy decks did not contain twos to sixes. This is why significance is rarely given to duplication of the lower numbers.

RUNES

What we now know as the runic alphabet appears to have grown from two separate sources: one magical and one literate. The precise meanings of these signs are now lost to us, as is the original reason for their creation. They are thought to have been used for divination or lot-casting, and it is fairly certain that they contributed to the magical uses of later runic alphabets. ⬧ The popularity of the runes diminished somewhat after they became a focus of interest for German scholars connected with the Nazi movement during the 1930s. What began as a revival of Teutonic folklore became so misapplied by the Nazis that the runes fell into disfavor. ⬧ By the mid-1980s, however, the runes had regained their popularity as both a divinatory system and a tool to increase self-knowledge.

Origins of the Runes

Runic inscriptions
Eleventh-century carvings of runic characters on stone, found near Uppsala in Sweden.

The word "rune" evolved from Germanic and Gothic roots meaning "secret" or "mystery." At one time it also meant "poem," but there is little evidence of a literary use of the runes in early times. Whatever their original meaning, the development of the rune symbols was prompted by the easiest way of carving them in wood or stone, and straight lines were simple signs that could be made by the most primitive of craftspeople.

The origin and purpose of the runes are marked with controversy. Their origin is certainly from the ancient tribes of northern Europe and they may have been used originally either as an alphabet or as a magical symbolic language. Differences between the sets of images developed across northern Europe, and extra signs were added, so that runic alphabets ranged from 28 to 32 runes, according to the region. As Christianity took hold in western Europe during the eleventh and twelfth centuries, the use of runes declined and they were banned because of their association with paganism. However, the runes continued to flourish in Scandinavia and the Baltic regions.

The futhork runes

The most popular runes for divination purposes are the Germanic futhork runes, which are based on the sounds of the initials of the first six characters, "f," "u," "t," "h," "o," "r," and "k." The futhork is divided into three sets of eight, or "aettirs," making 24 runes in all. Each of these aettirs is named after a Norse deity. Freya, the goddess of love, lust, war, and death, presides over the first aettir. The second aettir is named after Hagal, the guardian of the gods and goddesses. Finally Tiu, the god of law, justice, the sky, and war, is chief of the third aettir. The runes of each aettir contain qualities of their corresponding deities.

Ancient Norse legend attributes the invention of these powerful images to the chief Norse god or warrior-king, Odin. It is said that he hung from the world tree, Yggdrasil, for nine days and nine nights in order to gain the knowledge of the runes. Each of the rune characters contains a double meaning: an outer, material meaning and an inner, spiritual one.

Runes and Tarot

The image of Odin hanging from Yggdrasil, the world tree, has a strong link with the "hanged man" card in the tarot, and many sources suggest that the tarot image represents Odin.

Odin
*Norse god of battle,
death, and inspiration,
he was the chief of the
Aesir family of gods,
and also called the
All Father.*

FREYA'S AETTIR

The first aettir was named after the goddess Freya. She was also known as the Lady of the Vanir. The Vanir consisted of the second Germanic family of deities, with the Aesir being the most important. The Vanir deities were called upon for rain, fertility, sun, good harvest, and good winds. Freya is goddess of love, lust, war, and death. Her brother Frey is god of spring, harvest, and fertility.

Feoh
Meaning: cattle.
Phonetic equivalent: F.
Keywords: concern with physical and financial needs; prosperity, money, promotion, self-esteem.
Talisman: for achieving a goal, starting new enterprises; for money, business, promotion, and finding a job.

Ur
Meaning: wild ox.
Phonetic equivalent: U.
Keywords: sexuality, fertility, the unconscious, passion, vitality, instinct, wildness, and primitive inclinations.
Talisman: to increase sexual potency and energy; for hunting, and to strengthen the will.

Thorn

Meaning: giant.
Phonetic equivalent: TH (as in "think").
Keywords: hardship, a painful occurrence, discipline; knowledge, introspection, and deep thought.
Talisman: aid for discipline, study, meditation, resolving a bad situation.

Oss

Meaning: Odin.
Phonetic equivalent: A (as in "all").
Keywords: justice; a shaman, authority figure, leader; mind–body balance; clairvoyance.
Talisman: for help in divination, magic, in making wise decisions; for success and leadership.

Rit

Meaning: journey.
Phonetic equivalent: R.
Keywords: journey, quest, progress, life lessons, pilgrimage, change, and destiny.
Talisman: protection for travelers, to bring about change, ease a situation, and to reconnect.

Kaon

Meaning: torch.
Phonetic equivalent: C (as in "cat").
Keywords: creativity, inspiration, wisdom, insight, and the solution to a problem.
Talisman: for aid in study, creative inspiration; fertility; and dispelling anxiety and fear.

Gifu

Meaning: gift.
Phonetic equivalent: G (as in "girl").
Keywords: gift, generosity, unexpected good fortune, relationship, love, and partnership.
Talisman: to find or strengthen a relationship; to bring luck and fertility.

Wunna

Meaning: glory.
Phonetic equivalent: W.
Keywords: recognition, success, reward, joy, bliss, contentment, and the achievement of goals.
Talisman: for the completion of a task, success in an endeavor; and to motivate.

Freya's Aettir—Meanings

Each rune in Freya's aettir has a different set of meanings. These differ further depending on whether they fall face up or face down.

Feoh

Face up: possessions, earned income, and good fortune; abundance, financial strength in the present or near future; success and happiness; social success; energy, foresight, and fertility.

Face down: loss of personal property, esteem, or something that one has tried hard to keep; failure of some kind; greed, stupidity, dullness, poverty, slavery, and bondage.

Ur

Face up: physical strength, haste, and untamed potential; a period of great energy and health; freedom, energy, action, strength, tenacity, understanding, and courage; deeper wisdom and greater insight.

Face down: domination by others; weakness, obsession, and misdirected energy; sickness, inconsistency, and ignorance; brutality, rashness, callousness, and violence.

Thorn

Face up: a directed force of destruction or defense, conflict; instinctive will and the regenerative impulse; a tendency toward change; purging or a cleansing fire; male sexuality and fertilization.

Face down: danger, vulnerability, compulsion, betrayal, and dullness; evil, torment, spite, lies, malice, and hatred; a bad man or woman.

Oss

Face up: a revealing communication, message, or insight. Inspiration, enthusiasm, speech, clear vision, and the power of words and naming; blessings and getting good advice; good health.

Face down: misunderstanding, manipulation by others, delusion, and boredom; vanity and pomposity; being at the mercy of someone with their own selfish or negative agenda.

Rit

Face up: travel, in many senses; change of lifestyle; a journey, vacation, house move, or change of place or setting; seeing a larger perspective; deciding on the right move to make.
Face down: crisis, rigidity, stasis, injustice, and irrationality; disruption, dislocation, demotion, and delusion; imprisonment and being caged.

Kaon

Face up: a revelation, knowledge, new vision, creativity, inspiration, and technical ability; vital transformation and regeneration, the power to create one's own reality together with the power of knowledge; new strength, fresh ideas, a feeling of imaginative hope.
Face down: disease, breakup, instability, and lack of new ideas and creativity; nakedness, exposure, disillusionment, false desires; dissolution, hopelessness, falsehood, feelings of despair.

Gifu

Face up: gifts, in the sense of both sacrifices and generous acts; a sense of balance and equality; important matters in relation to exchanges, contracts, personal relationships, marriage, and partnerships.
Face down: greed, loneliness, dependence, and oversacrifice; obligation, one-sided generosity; poverty, privation, spiritual and emotional hunger, and bribery.

Wunna

Face up: pleasure, joy, and comfort; prosperity, fellowship, and harmony; appreciation, but a possibility of going to extremes; if restrained, the meaning is general success and recognition of one's worth.
Face down: sorrow, strife, and alienation; delirium and intoxication; being possessed by higher forces; wild and impractical enthusiasm; rage.

Yer, the harvest
The rune symbolizing the yearly cycle of plowing, planting, tilling, and weeding, leading to fruitfulness and produce.

HAGAL'S AETTIR
The second aettir is named after Hagal or Heimdal, one of the Aesir deities, who is considered to be the guardian of the gods and goddesses. He was said to be father of humankind, and is also the god of security. Hagal was the deadly enemy of Loki, the god of mischief, and owned a horn called "Gjallarhorn" and a sword called "Manhead." He was born of nine sisters, who had teeth of gold. He was said to have the ability to hear grass growing and to see at a distance of 100 miles (160 kilometers), day or night.

Hagal
Meaning: hail, health.
Phonetic equivalent: H.
Keywords: disaster, destruction, a sudden loss, ordeal, clearance, testing, a karmic lesson, and drastic change.
Talisman: for removing unwanted influences and breaking repeated destructive patterns.

Naut
Meaning: need, necessity.
Phonetic equivalent: N.
Keywords: discontentment, obstacles, poverty, hardship, responsibility, impasse, and frustration.
Talisman: to fulfill a need; to turn a negative fate around.

Is

Meaning: ice.
Phonetic equivalent: I (as in "inch").
Keywords: withdrawal, rest, inactivity, blockage, | stagnation; potential, patience, and reflection.
Talisman: to stop a process; to give oneself breathing space.

Yer

Meaning: year, harvest.
Phonetic equivalent: Y (but may be used in place of J).
Keywords: change, the yearly cycle; reward, | motion, productivity, and inevitable development.
Talisman: to bring about change; for fertility and growth.

Yr

Meaning: yew tree.
Phonetic equivalent: El.
Keywords: change, initiation; confrontation of one's fears; turning point, death, and | transformation.
Talisman: to bring about profound change; to ease a life transition or extreme difficulty.

Peorth

Meaning: a dice cup.
Phonetic equivalent: P.
Keywords: change, rebirth, mystery, magic, divination, fertility, sexuality; new beginnings and | prophecy.
Talisman: to aid in divination and magic; fertility, easing childbirth, and enhancing psychic powers.

Aquizi

Meaning: protection
Phonetic equivalent: X, Z.
Keywords: protection, assistance, defense, warning, support; | a mentor and an ethical dilemma.
Talisman: for protection, hunting, and to build a defense.

Sig

Meaning: sun.
Phonetic equivalent: S.
Keywords: success, positive energy, increase, power, activity, fertility, | and health.
Talisman: for extra energy, strength, success, healing, optimism; drive, enthusiasm, fertility.

Hagal's Aettir—Meanings

The runes of Hagal's aettir have different sets of meanings. These differ further depending on whether they fall face up or face down.

Hagal

Face up: uncontrolled forces, either destructive acts of nature or the unconscious; tempering, a testing trial; a controlled crisis leading to completion; inner harmony.

Face down: a natural disaster or catastrophe; stagnation or loss of power; pain, loss, suffering, hardship, sickness, and crisis.

Naut

Face up: delays and restriction; resistance leading to strength or innovation; conflict, but the power of will to overcome it; endurance, survival, and determination; a time for great patience; facing fears.

Face down: constraint of freedom, distress, toil, drudgery, and laxity; necessity, want, deprivation, and poverty; an emotional hunger.

Is

Face up: a challenge or frustration; a psychological block to thought or creativity; activity, holding grievances; a standstill or a time to turn inward and to wait for what is to come or to seek clarity; this rune reinforces the meanings of other runes around it.

Face down: treachery, illusion, deceit, betrayal, guile, stealth, ambush, and plots; egomania, dullness, blindness, and dissipation.

Yer

Face up: the realization of the results of earlier efforts; a period of peace and happiness or a fruitful season after much hard work; a breakthrough after a period of stagnation; hopes and expectations of peace and prosperity.

Face down: a sudden or unexpected setback or a reversal of fortune; a major change in life; pointless repetition, bad timing, poverty, and unavoidable conflict.

Yr

Face up: the possibility of achieving set goals; strength, reliability, dependability, and trustworthiness; enlightenment and endurance; defense and protection.

Face down: confusion, destruction, dissatisfaction, and weakness; an inability to overcome the current issue.

Peorth

Face up: initiation; knowledge of one's destiny or of future matters; pertaining to the feminine; this rune is always of uncertain meaning and can indicate a secret matter, a mystery, hidden things, and occult abilities.

Face down: addiction, stagnation, loneliness, and malaise; lack of understanding; a sense of loss and of finality, endings, or death.

Aquizi

Face up: protection or a shield; an urge to shelter oneself or others; defense and warding off a threat; a connection with the gods, an awakening, or higher life; this rune can be used to channel energies appropriately and toward a higher good that transcends that of the solitary self.

Face down: hidden danger; consumption by the divine forces or the loss of a divine link; a taboo or warning; a turning away or that which repels.

Sig

Face up: success, the achievement of goals, and honor; the life force or health; a time when power becomes available for positive change; victory, health, and contact between the higher self and the unconscious.

Face down: false goals, bad advice, the illusion of success, delusions of grandeur, gullibility, despair, or the loss of goals; destruction, retribution, justice, and the casting down of vanity and egotism.

The rune Eh
The nineteenth rune's literal meaning is horse, one of the most sacred animals of the Elder faith of northern Europe.

TIU'S AETTIR

The third aettir is named after Tiu, Tyr, or Tiwaz, another member of the Aesir deities, who was known as Skyfather. Tiu was one-handed, having sacrificed one of his arms chaining Fenrir, the giant wolf, who tried to destroy the world. He was god of justice, council, loyalty, the sky, and war. He was a battle god and to have him on your side always meant victory. Tiu's name is still retained in the weekday Tuesday.

Tiu
Meaning: Tiu.
Phonetic equivalent: T.
Keywords: duty, discipline, responsibility; self-sacrifice, conflict, strength, a wound, physicality, and the warrior path.
Talisman: to protect in the material sphere; to give victory or strength or to strengthen the will; for healing a wound.

Birca
Meaning: birch.
Phonetic equivalent: B.
Keywords: healing, fertility, new beginnings, growth, conception, plenty, and clearance.
Talisman: for healing (especially infections); for a good harvest, to achieve conception; for making a fresh start.

Eh

Meaning: horse
Phonetic equivalent: E (as in "egg").
Keywords: motion, transportation; a call for divine aid; energy, power, communication, will; recklessness.

Talisman: for power; communication and transportation; to deliver a spell.

Man

Meaning: man, humankind.
Phonetic equivalent: M.
Keywords: significator, the human race, self, family, community, relationships, and social concerns.

Talisman: to represent a person or group of people; to establish social relationships.

Lagu

Meaning: water, sea.
Phonetic equivalent: L.
Keywords: emotions, deep fears, the unconscious mind, things hidden; revelations, intuition, and counseling.

Talisman: for enhancing psychic abilities, confronting fears, stabilizing mental or emotional disorders, uncovering the hidden.

Ing

Meaning: people.
Phonetic equivalent: NG.
Keywords: work, productivity, bounty; community, balance, and connection with the land.

Talisman: for fertility, successful farming, growth, general health, and balance.

Odal

Meaning: inherited property.
Phonetic equivalent: O.
Keywords: property, land, inheritance, home, the family name; legacy, synthesis, and a sense of belonging.

Talisman: for acquiring property; to complete a project, and to bring strength to family ties.

Dag

Meaning: day.
Phonetic equivalent: D (pronounced "th," as in "this").
Keywords: happiness, brightness, success; activity, a fulfilling lifestyle, and satisfaction.

Talisman: to bring a positive outcome to any venture.

Tiu's Aettir—Meanings

The meanings of each rune in Tiu's aettir differ, depending on whether they fall face up or face down.

Tiu

Face up: honor, justice, leadership, authority; analysis, rationality; knowing where one's true strengths lie; willing self-sacrifice; success in competition or legal matters.

Face down: the blocking of one's energy and creative flow; mental paralysis, overanalysis, oversacrifice, injustice, and imbalance; strife, war, and conflict.

Birca

Face up: birth, general fertility, mental and physical personal growth, and liberation; the regenerative power and light of spring; promise of new beginnings and new growth; arousal of desire; a love affair or new birth.

Face down: family problems or domestic troubles; anxiety about someone close; carelessness, abandon, and loss of control.

Eh

Face up: transportation, movement, and change for the better; progressive gradual development and steady progress; harmony, teamwork, trust, and loyalty; an ideal marriage or partnership; this rune confirms and accents those around it.

Face down: craving a change; feeling restless or confined; even face down, this is not really a negative rune.

Man

Face up: the self, the individual, singularity; and an individual plurality such as the human race; one's attitude toward others and their attitudes toward oneself; friends and enemies, and the social order; the promise of some sort of imminent aid or cooperation.

Face down: a period of self-delusion, feelings of depression, mortality, and blindness; cunning, slyness, manipulation, craftiness, and calculation; no help or cooperation is promised.

Lagu

Face up: dreams, fantasies, mysteries, the unknown, the hidden, the deep, and the underworld; flow of liquid or life, water, sea, a fertility source, and the healing power of renewal; life energy and organic growth; imagination, intuition, and psychic matters.

Face down: a period of confusion and distressing illusions; wrong decisions and poor judgement; lack of creativity and the feeling of being in a rut; little energy or growth.

Ing

Face up: a resting stage, a time of relief with no feelings of anxiety; the tying-up of loose ends and the freedom to move in a new direction; male fertility, gestation, and internal growth; common virtues and common sense.

Face down: impotence, stagnation, and movement without change; production, a time of toil, labor, and never-ending work.

Odal

Face up: inherited property or possessions; a house or a home; what is truly important to one; group order and prosperity; the land of one's birth; spiritual heritage, experience, and fundamental values.

Face down: the loss of systems and order; homelessness; feeling cut off from one's roots, family, friends, and inheritance; bad karma or the negative results of past negative actions; prejudice, clannishness, and provincialism.

Dag

Face up: a breakthrough, awakening, and awareness; daylight clarity as opposed to dark uncertainty; a period to plan or embark upon an enterprise; the power of the self; initiated change; hope and happiness; the ideal.

Face down: completion, ending, limit, coming full circle; uncertainty, stagnation, and hopelessness.

Pebbles
Washed and shaped by the elements, pebbles represent a sensitivity and closeness with the Earth that is unsurpassed by commercially made runestones.

THE RUNE READING
First acquire a set of runes made of wood, stone, or any other material of your choice. Available in most "New Age" shops, these can also be bought via the Internet. If you are skilled at making things, creating your own set of runes will be a rewarding and very direct way of getting to know each rune. You could paint or carve runes on small, flat pebbles with a craft tool to produce a personalized set of stones. Then make or find a soft bag in which to keep them.

FEOH

LAGU

YR

Past, present, and future layout
The question asked was: "Will we sell our house next month?" The three rune stones thrown were Feoh (face up), Lagu (face down), and Yr (face up).

The past
The Feoh rune indicates earned income, good fortune, and financial strength in the near future. So we can presume that the house was and is valuable, particularly in the current housing market, and is potentially a great asset to the sellers.

The present
Lagu indicates a period of confusion in one's life, the making of wrong decisions and poor judgements, a lack of creativity, and feelings of being in a rut. Being face down, it represents the worry and uncertainty of the questioner. The sellers are in financial difficulties and it is important that they make a sale soon.

The future
Yr signifies that you have set your sights on a target and can achieve your goal. Representing strength endurance, and protection, this is a happy rune for the future. It appears as though the answer to the question is "Yes," and that the questione wish can be achieved

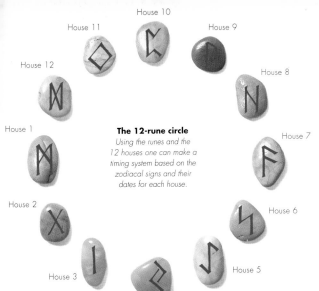

The 12-rune circle
Using the runes and the 12 houses one can make a timing system based on the zodiacal signs and their dates for each house.

House 10
House 11
House 9
House 12
House 8
House 1
House 7
House 2
House 6
House 3
House 5
House 4

The 12 Houses

House 1 Aries, March 21 to April 20, Man (face down).

House 2 Taurus, April 21 to May 21, Gifu (face down).

House 3 Gemini, May 22 to June 21, Is (face up).

House 4 Cancer, June 22 to July 23, Yer (face up).

House 5 Leo, July 24 to August 23, Yr (face up).

House 6 Virgo, August 24 to September 23, Sig (face down).

House 7 Libra, September 24 to October 22, Oss (face up).

House 8 Scorpio, October 23 to November 22, Hagal (face up).

House 9 Sagittarius, November 23 to December 21, Ur (face up).

House 10 Capricorn, December 22 to January 20, Peorth (face up).

House 11 Aquarius, January 21 to February 19, Ing (face up).

House 12 Pisces, February 20 to March 20, Dag (face up).

Reading the Rune Layouts

The throw

Before the throw hold the stones gently, close your eyes, and allow the power of the stones to enter your psyche. There is no hurry in divination.

Make yourself familiar with the 24 images by testing yourself daily. Choose a rune and recall as much of its meaning as possible before looking up its definition. Consider how the rune chosen reflects the nature and occurrences of your day.

The past, present, and future layout

This is the simplest reading. Shake the runes in the bag while thinking of your question, then take out three stones and shake them in your hands without looking at them, allowing them as much movement as you can; then throw them on a table. Place them from left to right in a row in the order that they fall. They represent the past, present, and future. If you must turn a rune over, remember that it was lying face down and interpret it accordingly. (See the sample reading on pages 110–11.)

The 12-rune circle

For a reading to give some idea of how someone's year will be, an adaptation of the astrological tarot spread is very effective (see the example on page 33). Shake the bag well, then set the runes in the order given below.

As the question "How will my year go?" was asked on September 6, we locate the present month in the sixth house, Virgo. The reading will move from the sixth house around the months in a counterclockwise direction.

August to September, Sig (face down): false goals and bad advice are signified; everything seems fine, but there is an underlying message that things are going wrong under the surface.

September to October, Oss (face up): inspiration, a message or insight helps sort out last month's mistakes.

October to November, Hagal (face up): uncontrolled forces or destructive acts of nature, especially weather; make sure that your house roof is sound.

November to December, Ur (face up): good health, energy, and tenacity are shown, indicating that it is a good time for doing important jobs.

December to January, Peorth (face up): uncertain meaning; a secret mystery involving a female family member.

January to February, Ing (face up): a resting stage; a time of relief with no anxiety, when loose ends are tied and one is free to move in a new direction; a month of welcome relaxation.

Runes and the Tarot

We can borrow many of the well-known tarot spreads in order to do rune readings, such as the Celtic Cross, the planetary, and the astrological spreads.

February to March, Dag (face up): things begin to move in the direction you want.

March to April, Man (face down): setbacks through the actions of a dishonest person are indicated.

April to May, Gifu (face down): greed, loneliness, privation, and bribery; there is something going on that you should know about.

May to June, Is (face up): a challenge or frustration; the probable outcome of the previous month, the denouement.

June to July, Yer (face up): the results of earlier efforts are realized; a fruitful season; hopes of peace and prosperity; recovery from the events of April to June.

July to August, Yr (face up): you have set your sights on a possible target and can achieve your goals; strength, reliability, dependability, and trustworthiness are shown, as well as endurance and enlightenment; the year will end on a high note.

THE AETTIR AND HORARY CLOTHS

The other method of doing a reading is to throw the runes onto a board or cloth that is marked with definite areas of meaning. You can, of course, make your own board or cloth. If you're not too skilled with a needle, maybe a talented member of the family would make you an embroidered rune cloth. If you're not artistic, persuade the family Michelangelo to paint you a board to your specifications. The runes are great decorative motifs, and there will inevitably be some that you prefer.

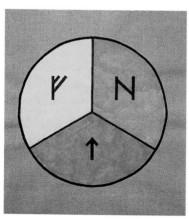

The aettir cloth

Using the aettir cloth, the runes are interpreted as follows.
Runes falling in:
Freya: these specifically refer to matters of love, creativity, and happiness.
Hagal: these refer to business, achievement, success, and money—that is, the things that one desires.
Tiu: these relate to the mind and the spirit, deeper matters, and one's life philosophy and ethics.

The horary cloth

The horary cloth is divided into 12 houses (see diagram on p116). Select the runes from the bag and throw them onto the board. The runes will describe events that are related only to the houses in which they fall. If they land face downward, they will denote hidden events. If they cross a line, choose the house that has the most of it covered. Runes outside the square are not read.

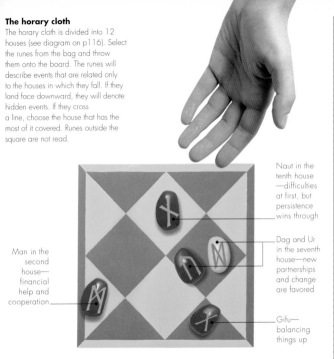

Naut in the tenth house —difficulties at first, but persistence wins through

Dag and Ur in the seventh house—new partnerships and change are favored

Man in the second house— financial help and cooperation

Gifu— balancing things up

A sample reading

Question: "I wish to set up my own business— is the time right at the moment?" Six runes were thrown, with five landing on the board.

Man in the second house: aid or cooperation in the area of finance and possessions.

Gifu in the fifth house: gifts, sacrifices, and generous acts; balancing between what one receives and what one gives.

Naut in the tenth house: delays and restriction; conflict, but the power to overcome it.

Ur in the seventh house: a period of great energy; freedom.

Dag in the seventh house: breakthrough, awakening, awareness; self-initiated change.

Summing up: "OK, the time's right, but it's going to be hard work."

Rune Reading Interpretations

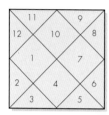

The horary cloth

This is quite easy to make, either painted on board or embroidered on cloth, and adds much to the quality of the reading.

If you choose one of the following layouts, it would be good if you took the time to design and create your own cloth to make it more meaningful and permanent.

The aettir cloth

A cloth or board with a circular design is good for the "aettir" throw. It should be around 14–18 inches (35–45 centimeters) in diameter, otherwise many of the runes will fall outside the circle. Divide the circle into three 120° segments. These three segments represent the three aettirs, and each

should be decorated or marked with the appropriate rune: Freya, Hagal, and Tiu. Some intricate Celtic patterns would make it really special.

In making the throw on the aettir cloth, gently shake your rune bag and take out a small handful of runes, perhaps six or seven (but just guess, since it is not necessary to be exact). With your hand raised—but not too high—above the center of the cloth, release the runes and begin the reading. Runes falling into the Freya segment refer to matters of love, creativity, and happiness; runes falling in Hagal refer to business, achievement, success, and money; and runes in Tiu relate to the mind, spirit, deeper life matters, and one's life philosophy and ethics.

In this method, runes that fall face downward are usually read as hidden events or things that we have not yet admitted to ourselves. Runes that fall outside the circle denote events that are approaching in the distant future, related to the circle segment nearest to which they have fallen.

The horary cloth

The ancient square charts that we see in medieval manuscripts are still sometimes used in horary astrology. There is a decorative quality about them that gives a feeling of magic to the reading.

Such a board works well with a rune cast: the straight lines making the 12 sections, square and triangular, are sympathetic to the basic linear quality of runic images. As with the previous rune cloth, the board can be colored and embellished, and should be about 16–20 inches (40–50 centimeters) square. The various astrological houses and the runic meanings are a simplified version of the spread used in the tarot.

The 12 Houses and Their Significance	
House 1 Self	**House 7** Partnership and marriage
House 2 Possessions and finances	**House 8** Shared money and inheritances
House 3 Communication	**House 9** Philosophy and beliefs
House 4 The home	**House 10** Career and position
House 5 Creativity and love affairs	**House 11** Friends
House 6 Work and health	**House 12** Sacrifices and helping others

I CHING

The *I Ching*, or "Book of Changes," was devised by a legendary Chinese sage named Fu Hsi, who lived over 4,500 years ago. He created the *I Ching*'s unbroken and broken lines to represent the polarities of creation: unbroken, positive—*yang*; and broken, negative—*yin*. With these, as well as his direct observations of the earth, sky, and living creatures, he devised the eight basic trigrams that became the basis of the *I Ching*. Around 1150 BC, King Wen, the progenitor of the Chou Dynasty, composed the original version of the *I Ching*. During his seven-year imprisonment by Emperor Shin Chou (who was jealous of his popularity), King Wen created the 64 six-lined hexagrams, and a commentary for each. After his death, his son, the Duke of Chou, added commentaries on the individual lines of the hexagrams. These became the basis of the *I Ching* prediction system.

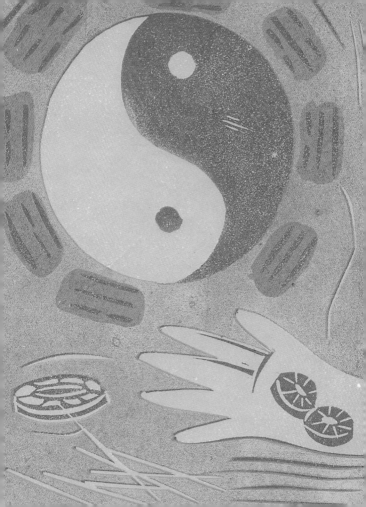

The Trigrams

Ch'ien

The three unbroken lines of the trigram Ch'ien represent heaven and the yang side of nature.

The unbroken line began as a simple image for "Yes" in Chinese divination. It is now called *yang*, representing "heaven," and corresponds to the positive, active, and masculine side of nature. The broken line stood at first for "No," and is now called *yin*, representing "earth," or "the yielding," and corresponds to the negative, feminine, passive side of nature.

In the table below we can see the make-up of the trigrams that will later go to form the 64 hexagrams. The trigrams are formed from three broken or unbroken lines, and each kind of line has significance at various placings. The lines are grouped in threes in eight possible permutations.

The Eight Trigrams

Trigram	Name	Attribute	Image	Family
☰	Ch'ien	Heaven	Active	Father
☱	Tui	Lake	Joyful	Youngest daughter
☲	Li	Fire	Clinging	Second daughter
☳	Chen	Thunder	Arousing	Eldest son
☴	Sun	Wind	Gentle	Eldest daughter
☵	K'an	Water	Dangerous	Second son
☶	Ken	Mountain	Immovable	Youngest son
☷	K'un	Earth	Responsive	Mother

These eight trigrams were the basis of an early form of divination, and are often pictured arranged in a circle around the interlocking yin-yang symbol.

Each has a name and is further described by an attribute, an image, and a family relationship.

It is important to remember that the trigrams are symbols of change and do not represent static conditions. Each trigram is constantly changing into another. Studying the trigrams separately will be of great help in a later understanding of the fuller depth of the complete hexagram.

The eight trigrams

Each of the eight trigrams is made up of a combination of the two types of lines in different ways, covering the complete *yang* trigram to the complete *yin* trigram. The trigram is read from the bottom up, line by line, to give an understanding of the continual change from one principle to the other.

Confucius and the *I Ching*

When Confucius became aware of the "Book of Changes," he was so impressed and used it so often that he wore out the leather thongs binding his copy three times.

Yarrow sticks

The traditional yarrow sticks, which are hard to find, can be replaced with oriental satay skewers from your local supermarket. Just remove the pointed ends.

CASTING METHODS

The standard texts of the *I Ching* are lengthy and quite obscure on first reading. Although the detail of the various "commentaries" is complex, with much symbolism, the principle is very simple. The traditional way of producing a reading is equally time-consuming, but there are several alternatives you can use that take only minutes to produce a good result.

Coins and cards

It is now possible to find replicas of traditional Chinese coins, which add authenticity to your coin throws. There are also several I Ching card decks that can be used, if preferred.

Doing a reading

The simplest way in which to do a reading is to use three ordinary coins. There is another, more elaborate, method that uses 50 "yarrow" sticks. Although this is conducive to a gently contemplative approach to a reading, it requires much practice and is best learned when one has gained more knowledge of the oracle. You can also buy *I Ching* "counters," or even packs of 64 cards (each card representing one hexagram) that can be used to do a reading. Because the *I Ching*'s structure is fundamentally "binary," to use a mathematical term (yin and yang), it is suitable for computer-based readings, too, and many software programs have been created for it. Whichever method you use, your main objective is to reveal a hexagram built from six lines from the bottom to the top. Once the hexagram has been created, the *I Ching* is consulted and the wisdom discovered.

The Line Symbols

One throw of the three coins will show you which line should be drawn, as illustrated in the following table.

Coin throw	The line	
3 tails	"Moving" yang	—o—
3 heads	"Moving" yin	—×—
2 tails, 1 head,	Yang	——
2 heads, 1 tail	Yin	– –

Heads or tails?
Make your decision concerning as to which side represents the "head" and "tail" and keep to that decision on all future readings.

The three-coin method

1 Take three coins of the same type, concentrate on the question on which you seek guidance, and throw all of the coins together, noting how they land. The primary object is to decide which side is *ying* and which *yang*. The coins should preferably have "head" and "tail" sides, and in this example we have chosen the head side as *yin* and the tail side as *yang*.

2 Draw the appropriate line symbol on a piece of paper (see box above). Repeat the process until you have six lines, drawing each appropriate line above the previous one. (The "moving" lines are initially read as if they were ordinary *yin* and *yang* lines.)

3 Once you have built your hexagram, any "moving" line is then reversed in meaning a "moving" *yin* line becomes a *yang* (unbroken) line and a "moving" *yang* line becomes a *yin* [broken] line.

4 Divide this final hexagram into the "top" three and the "bottom" three, and you will then be ready to find your hexagram from the key (see page 124).

1st hexagram with moving lines

2nd hexagram

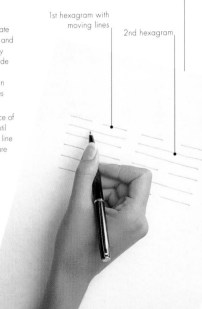

The Hexagram Tables

Having mentally divided the hexagram into upper and lower trigrams, take a look at the table below. Look along the top row until you find the image that matches your upper

trigram and make a mental note of the column that it heads. Then look down the left side of the table until you find the image that matches your bottom trigram. Trace your finger to the right

The 64 Hexagrams

	Ch'ien	Chen	K'an	Ken	K'un	Sun	Li	Tui
Ch'ien	Ch'ien 1	Ta Chuang 34	Hsu 5	Ta Ch'u 26	T'ai 11	Hsiao Ch'u 9	Ta Yu 14	Kuai 43
Chen	Wu Wang 25	Chen 51	Chun 3	I 27	Fu 24	I 42	Shih Ho 21	Sui 17
K'an	Sung 6	Hsieh 40	K'an 29	Meng 4	Shih 7	Huan 59	Wei Chi 64	K'un 47
Ken	Tun 33	Hsiao Kuo 62	Chien 39	Ken 52	Ch'ien 15	Chien 53	Lu 56	Hsien 31
K'un	P'i 12	Yu 16	Pi 8	Po 23	K'un 2	Kuan 20	Chin 35	Ts'ui 45
Sun	Kou 44	Heng 32	Ching 48	Ku 18	Sheng 46	Sun 57	Ting 50	Ta Kuo 28
Li	T'ung Jen 13	Feng 55	Chi Chi 63	Pi 22	Ming I 36	Chia Jen 37	Li 30	Ko 49
Tui	Lu 10	Kuei Mei 54	Chieh 60	Sun 41	Lin 19	Chung Fu 61	K'uei 38	Tui 58

along that row until it is directly below the top trigram. The square where the two lines merge gives the number of your hexagram. Now go to its commentary (see pages 126–41), which should be interpreted according to your question and state of mind.

There are normally three levels of interpretation, or approaches, you can take in making sense of the symbols, or regarding how they relate to your "self" or life. They are: your relationship with the world or a group on an intellectual-behavioral plane; your private, emotional reactions or relationship with one other person; and your spiritual situation or state of being on a broader scale or higher level.

Imagery in the *I Ching*

The imagery used in the *I Ching*, and the ideals upon which it was based, are from a time when people lived closer to nature and were more sensitive to its constant changes. From nature, they learned how to make judgements, and assessed themselves within its context. This encouraged the wisdom that leads to humility—sorely needed by humanity today.

Fu Hsi

The legendary sage Fu Hsi first developed the eight trigrams of the I Ching.

HEXAGRAMS 1 TO 16

The commentaries contained in the great translations of the *I Ching*, notably the version by Richard Wilhelm, are beautiful, but far too long, complex, and initially obscure to cover in this book. We have, therefore, given some indication of the meaning of each of the hexagrams, but recommend that, if your interest is stimulated, you acquire a copy of an original text.

1 Chi'en, The creative
HEAVEN *above,*
HEAVEN *below.*

2 K'un, The receptive
EARTH *above,*
EARTH *below.*

3 Chun, Difficulty
in the beginning
WATER *above,*
THUNDER *below.*

4 Meng, Youth
MOUNTAIN *above,*
WATER *below.*

5 Hsu, Waiting
WATER *above,*
HEAVEN *below.*

6 Sung, Conflict
HEAVEN *above,*
WATER *below.*

7 Shih, The army
EARTH *above,*
WATER *below.*

8 Pi, Union
WATER *above,*
EARTH *below.*

9 Hsiao Ch'u, Taming
the small powers
WIND *above,*
HEAVEN *below.*

10 Lu, Treading [conduct]
HEAVEN *above,*
LAKE *below.*

11 T'ai, Peace
EARTH *above,*
HEAVEN *below.*

12 P'i, Stagnation
HEAVEN *above,*
EARTH *below.*

13 T'ung Jen, Fellowship
with people
HEAVEN *above,*
FLAME *below.*

14 Ta Yu, Great
possessions
FLAME *above,*
HEAVEN *below.*

Difficulty at the beginning
*The first part of an enterprise is
the hardest. Just like young
shoots having to
withstand severe
winds and rain.*

15 Ch'ien, Modesty
EARTH *above,*
MOUNTAIN *below.*

16 Yu, Happiness
THUNDER *above,*
EARTH *below.*

I Ching **Hexagrams 1 to 16**

SECRETS OF DIVINATION

127

Hexagrams 1 to 16

Yin-yang
Feminine and masculine polarity lies at the heart of all I Ching prediction. One must be complemented by the other.

The following connotations have been given to the first 16 hexagrams as described below.

1 *Chi'en,* The creative
Persevere and tune your creative abilities into the celestial tides, i.e. spiritual levels. Complacency or arrogance will bring misfortune.

2 *K'un,* The receptive
Be aware of what others are saying and heed their advice. Yield to the call of duty and try to act with it in mind.

3 *Chun,* Difficulty in the beginning
Continue slowly and keep your objectives simple and small. Allow the big plan to evolve by itself. Deal with situations one at a time.

4 *Meng,* Youth
Be cautious and ensure that others are being honest with you. Check your facts carefully and only comment when you are confident of your facts.

5 *Hsu,* Waiting
Be patient and persistent and wait for the right moment. Be truthful with yourself and strong in your objectives.

6 *Sung,* Conflict
Take advice from more experienced people and guard your stability and security. Keep what you have rather than looking for something more.

7 *Shih,* The army
Show your leadership abilities and respect others. Build trust in people and be careful of arousing jealousy.

8 Pi, Union

Unite with others. Honesty and sincerity will lead to success if you cooperate. Doubts about your trustworthiness will lead to misfortune.

9 Hsiao Ch'u, Taming the small powers

Conserve your energy. Collect things that you will need to succeed in your future plans. Be patient and flexible.

10 Lu, Treading [conduct]

The situation is fraught with danger, but, by treading gently and carefully and acting with humility, after some careful planning, good fortune is indicated.

11 T'ai, Peace

Great relief after difficult times. A time of peace, prosperity, and good fortune. Be flexible, but true to yourself.

12 P'i, Stagnation

A time of stagnation and delay. Beware of pride combined with inability, as well as lack of harmony.

13 T'ung Jen, Fellowship with people

This suggests the support of a group. Partnerships and marriages will be successful if you act with honesty and flexibility. Cooperation is the key.

14 Ta Yu, Great possessions

A period of good fortune and respect from others. Return the respect and beware of laziness and arrogance.

15 Ch'ien, Modesty

Do not push forward aggressively. Act with humility to restore the balance between excess and dearth. Equality in partnerships will benefit you.

16 Yu, Happiness

Everything will go as you hoped, but do not be idle or negligent. Take opportunities as they arise and act with conviction, but do not be overconfident or immodest.

Nourishment
Good food nourishes, bad food harms the body. The symbol for nourishment represents the necessity of absorbing knowledge and learning.

HEXAGRAMS 17 TO 32 Traditionally, the

I Ching, when not in use, was kept wrapped in a special silk cloth and placed on a shelf not lower than the shoulders of a man standing erect. Before use, the hands were washed and the book unwrapped on a table, leaving the cloth between the book and the table in order to keep its purity untarnished.

17 *Sui*, Following
LAKE *above*,
THUNDER *below*.

18 *Ku*, Work after spoiling
MOUNTAIN *above*,
WIND *below*.

19 *Lin*, Approach
EARTH *above*,
LAKE *below*.

Observation
The immediate future may be difficult, but good fortune will follow if you take time to observe and plan.

20 *Kuan*, Observation
WIND *above*,
EARTH *below*.

**21 *Shih Ho*,
Biting through**
FLAME *above*,
THUNDER *below*.

22 Pi, Gracefulness
MOUNTAIN *above,*
FLAME *below.*

23 Po, Decay
[splitting apart]
MOUNTAIN *above,*
EARTH *below.*

24 Fu, Return [revival]
EARTH *above,*
THUNDER *below.*

25 Wu Wang, Innocence
[the unexpected]
HEAVEN *above,*
THUNDER *below.*

26 Ta Ch'u, Taming
the great powers
MOUNTAIN *above,*
HEAVEN *below.*

27 I, Nourishment
[the corners of the mouth]
MOUNTAIN *above,*
THUNDER *below.*

28 Ta Kuo,
Great excess
LAKE *above,*
WIND/WOOD *below.*

29 K'an,
The abysmal [pitfalls]
WATER *above,*
WATER *below.*

30 Li, Fire
FLAME *above,*
FLAME *below.*

31 Hsien,
Attraction [stimulation]
LAKE *above,*
MOUNTAIN *below.*

32 Heng, Duration
THUNDER *above,*
WIND *below.*

Hexagrams 17 to 32

Following

As with water in a stream of waves on a shore, go with the flow. A time to yield to other people's opinions.

Hexagrams 17 to 32 have commentaries that are summarized below. These names generally describe activity of one kind or another.

17 *Sui*, Following

Appreciate the great fortune around you. Use any period of decline to strengthen yourself and prepare for future opportunities.

18 *Ku*, Work after spoiling

Take time to make decisions, act carefully. Don't make new commitments. Avoid partnership decisions.

19 *Lin*, Approach

Your troubles will disappear and recognition will follow if you treat others kindly and modestly. Make the most of any success while it lasts.

20 *Kuan*, Observation

You will need the support of others. Be patient, plan, and take the time to observe and examine the behavior of both yourself and others.

21 *Shih Ho*, Biting through

Be strong and clear in your objectives and you will succeed. Avoid being bad-tempered or speaking harsh words.

22 *Pi*, Gracefulness

Ensure that you do not obscure the reality of the future with rose-colored spectacles. Firm, but flexible, action will result in prosperity.

23 *Po*, Decay [splitting apart]

Your current difficulties will soon end in a cycle of natural regeneration. Be patient and prepare for better times to come.

24 Fu, Return [revival]

Your present troubles, sadness, and confusion will soon give way to positive changes. Great patience is required.

25 Wu Wang, Innocence

Be prepared for unexpected events and be flexible in dealing with them when they occur. Act with truth and honor and without greed, ambition, or desire.

26 Ta Ch'u, Taming the great powers

You will need to do considerable work in order to win over, rather than subdue, those who try to oppose you.

27 I, Nourishment

You will succeed if you act with moderation and humility. Seek advice from the wise, but act unselfishly.

28 Ta Kuo, Great excess

Your situation will improve with patience. Evaluate your strengths and weaknesses when working out an appropriate course of action.

29 K'an, The abysmal [pitfalls]

Conserve your energy and don't try to deal with all of the difficulties that confront you. Find the natural course and follow it.

30 Li, Fire

Cooperative ventures will succeed. Be calm and self-controlled, and focus on your plans. You must be flexible, but make no changes unless it is absolutely necessary.

31 Hsien, Attraction [stimulation]

Be sensitive to others and stay resolved. Be receptive to new commitments. Assist and protect those who are weaker.

32 Heng, Duration

By maintaining continuity during a time of change you will end a difficult situation. Partnerships and marriage will endure and strengthen over time.

Retreat

It is best to withdraw so as not to exhaust oneself. Not as the flight of a weak person, but as the voluntary withdrawal of a strong one.

HEXAGRAMS 33 TO 48 The decision on

how to word a question in order to get the clearest answer is of great importance when throwing the *I Ching*. "Either/or" questions should be avoided; it is almost impossible to elicit answers to them. If a choice must be made between two options, it is best to focus on one only and ask what would be the outcome if that was the direction in which one was to proceed.

33 Tun, Retreat [withdrawal]
HEAVEN *above,*
MOUNTAIN *below.*

34 Ta Chuang,
The power of the great
THUNDER *above,*
HEAVEN *below.*

35 Chin, Progress
FLAME *above,*
EARTH *below.*

36 Ming I,
Darkening of the light
EARTH *above,*
FLAME *below.*

37 Chia Jen,
The family [the clan]
WIND *above,*
FLAME *below.*

38 K'uei, Opposition
FLAME *above*,
LAKE *below*.

39 Chien, Obstruction
WATER *above*,
MOUNTAIN *below*.

40 Hsieh, Liberation
THUNDER *above*,
WATER *below*.

41 Sun, Decrease
MOUNTAIN *above*,
LAKE *below*.

42 I, Increase
WIND *above*,
THUNDER *below*.

43 Kuai, Breakthrough
[resoluteness]
LAKE *above*,
HEAVEN *below*.

44 Kou, Encountering
HEAVEN *above*,
WIND *below*.

45 Ts'ui, Gathering
LAKE *above*,
EARTH *below*.

46 Sheng, Ascending
EARTH *above*,
WIND/WOOD *below*.

Darkening

*One must hide one's light in order
to make one's will prevail at
the right time. The light
is veiled, but not
extinguished.*

47 K'un, Oppression
LAKE *above*,
WATER *below*.

48 Ching,
The well
WATER *above*,
WIND/WOOD *below*.

Hexagrams 33 to 48

Increase

Enjoy smooth good fortune—it is time to get on the move. Long-distance travel in all senses of the word is favored.

The *I Ching* commentaries have given the following connotations to hexagrams 33 to 48.

33 Tun, Retreat [withdrawal]

The time for an orderly withdrawal—a sensible reaction to an impossible situation. Do not confront those who oppose you. Conserve your energies.

34 Ta Chuang,
The power of the great

A period of progress and good fortune. Others will be influenced by you, so act justly and wisely. Ensure that your success does not offend the less fortunate.

35 Chin, Progress

This is a good time for business and cooperative ventures. Act justly and modestly in order to win the enthusiasm and support of others.

36 Ming I, Darkening of the light

Things may not be going well, but do not become downhearted. Be careful whom you trust and act with caution. Be patient and make plans.

37 Chia Jen, The family [the clan]

Do not act in isolation, but in close rapport with your family and friends. Act sensitively and with respect.

38 K'uei, Opposition

Opposition, fighting, and contradictions are indicated. Look for constructive ways to bring about unification.

39 Chien, Obstruction

Although difficulties surround you, they are part of an essential process. Be constant in your objectives, but do not use force to achieve them.

40 *Hsieh*, Liberation

Conditions begin to improve. Deal with your difficulties quickly, but gently. Learn lessons, but do not have regrets.

41 *Sun*, Decrease

Avoid excesses and preserve the things that you have. Be restrained, but malleable, and act with sincerity.

42 *I*, Increase

A good time for increased activity, prosperity, and journeys. Share your good fortune and do not take advantage of others.

43 *Kuai*, Breakthrough [resoluteness]

Accept pitfalls and take action calmly. Act justly, with honor, and be watchful. Avoid forcing a situation.

44 *Kou*, Encountering

Do not follow someone else blindly. Be wary of difficult or dangerous situations and people. Act in an honest and upright manner.

45 *Ts'ui*, Gathering

A sympathetic relationship requires a gathering together with others. It also means gather your resources and accept good advice. Be prepared for testing times.

46 *Sheng*, Ascending

Although growth may take time, it will reap success and good rewards. Be prepared to work hard to consolidate your gains.

47 *K'un*, Oppression

Use your inner resolve to face the difficulties ahead. Losses will reveal what is truly important. Be quiet and watchful for deception and false flattery.

48 *Ching*, The well

The well is signified by the depth of your understanding based on past experience. Share this understanding to ensure you stay on a natural path. Things are good, but watch out for change.

The cauldron

This hexagram's combination of flames above and wood and wind below shows that all things are in order and there is stability and unobstructed flow.

HEXAGRAMS 49 TO 64
In China, traditionally, important personages face south when granting interviews. Therefore, the *I Ching* should be granted the same respect and importance and be placed on a table facing south, with the enquirer facing north. Before the reading is done, light a little incense and make three kowtows (or bows) to the "Book of Changes."

49 Ko, Revolution
LAKE *above,*
FLAME *below.*

50 Ting, The cauldron
FLAME *above,*
WIND/WOOD *below.*

51 Chen,
Thunder [shock]
THUNDER *above,*
THUNDER *below.*

52 Ken, Keeping still
MOUNTAIN *above,*
MOUNTAIN *below.*

53 Chien, Gradual development
WIND/WOOD *above,*
MOUNTAIN *below.*

54 Kuei Mei,
The marrying maiden
THUNDER *above,*
LAKE *below.*

55 Feng, Greatness
THUNDER *above,*
FLAME *below.*

56 Lu, Traveling
FLAME *above,*
MOUNTAIN *below.*

57 Sun, The gentle
[the penetrating]
WIND/WOOD *above,*
WIND/WOOD *below.*

58 Tui, Joyousness
LAKE *above,*
LAKE *below.*

59 Huan, Dispersion
WIND *above,*
WATER *below.*

60 Chieh, Limitation
WATER *above,*
LAKE *below.*

Keeping still

*The mountain signifies rest; one
should be still and unmoving.
It is a time for indifference
to worldly gain and
firm maintenance
of one's beliefs.*

61 Chung Fu,
Inner truthfulness
WIND *above,*
LAKE *below.*

63 Chi Chi,
After completion
WATER *above,*
FLAME *below.*

62 Hsiao Kuo,
Small successes
THUNDER *above,*
MOUNTAIN *below.*

64 Wei Chi,
Before completion
FLAME *above,*
WATER *below.*

SECRETS OF DIVINATION

139

Hexagrams 49 to 64

Thunder

A shock excites a striving to break away from suppression. Now is the time to overcome difficulties and achieve ambition.

Summaries of the connotations for hexagrams 49 to 64 of the *I Ching* are encapsulated in the following descriptions.

49 Ko, Revolution

Change should bring good opportunities. Resist change for the sake of mercenary interests and act carefully and with sincerity.

50 Ting, The cauldron

Material and spiritual success surround you. Maintain this harmony and your understanding of the world to enable new projects to progress well.

51 Chen, Thunder [shock]

A short period of upset should be followed by a time of success. Be wary of idle gossip.

52 Ken, Keeping still

This is a time for waiting and extreme patience. Pay attention to existing plans and partnerships rather than making new ones.

53 Chien, Gradual development

Work slowly, but surely, toward your objectives. If you make your plans carefully, the future will be bright.

54 Kuei Mei, The marrying maiden

Do not be not seduced by the superficial or the short term, but look for truth and objectivity. Beware of becoming involved in a potentially unmanageable situation.

55 Feng, Greatness

Good fortune, abundance, and prosperity surround you. Use them to prepare for more frugal times.

56 *Lu*, Traveling

The start of an important journey is indicated. Make sure of each step before taking the next. Remember that any attempts to reach your destination too quickly will fail.

57 *Sun*, The gentle [the penetrating]

Be steadfast, but don't push too hard—go with the wind. Act honorably.

58 *Tui*, Joyousness

This is a time of emotional happiness. Your joy and inner strength will attract others to you. Behave modestly and avoid arrogance and gossip.

59 *Huan*, Dispersion

Do not be deflected from your path. Conserve your resources and remain self-disciplined, as well as heeding others' needs.

60 *Chieh*, Limitation

Work within limitations and calmly use them to further your progress. Act wisely and think ahead.

61 *Chung Fu*, Inner truthfulness

Learn to understand yourself and your life: your peace lies within you. Sharing and communicating with others will bring success.

62 *Hsiao Kuo*, Small successes

Know your limitations and work within that framework. Pay attention to detail because success will come in small ways. Do not be overambitious. Modesty and conscientiousness will achieve results.

63 *Chi Chi*, After completion

There is good fortune, but this is not a time to sit back and rest on your laurels. Consolidate gains, act with caution, and strive to attain a balance.

64 *Wei Chi*, Before completion

It is unwise to act prematurely. Be patient and avoid disputes because the transition from confusion to order is not yet complete. You are following the right path.

GEOMANCY

The word "geomancy" means any system of divination related to manipulation of earth. Although the exact origins of astrological geomancy are unknown, a system of geomancy linking astrological symbols with figures formed from holes poked in the soil was popular during the Renaissance. It is similar to the casting of lots referred to in early Latin and Greek texts, and may have been practiced by desert nomads who made marks in the sand which they interpreted to answer questions of personal concern. The 16 geomantic archetypes bear a close relationship to the archetypal symbols of the planets and zodiacal signs used in astrology.

Geomantic Figures, Their Planets, and Meanings

Below are 16 geomantic figures, and their corresponding planets and zodiacal signs. The 16 figures can be grouped into eight complementary pairs, which function like negative opposites of each other.

Moon
In astrology the Moon is the symbol of the populace and the family. In geomancy this may extend to popular taste and conventional attitude.

Fortuna major
Leo/Sun, gold.
Great fortune, wealth, and success; internal aid.

Fortuna minor
Leo/Sun, gold.
Lesser fortune; protection or guidance; external aid.

Via
Cancer/Moon, silver.
Way, street, or journey; the path of initiation.

Populus
Cancer/Moon, silver.
People and community; a congregation or crowd.

Acquisito
Sagittarius/Jupiter, tin.
Acquisition: to receive, gain, or add to.

Amissio
Taurus/Venus, copper.
Loss: something removed or lost.

Conjunctio
Virgo/Mercury, quicksilver.
Union, joining, marriage, and conjunction.

Carcer
Capricorn/Saturn, lead.
Prison, restrictions, confinement, or delays.

Where one figure of a pair has a single dot, its complement has two dots.

The figures are listed next to their complements below, along with their associated metals, planets, zodiacal signs, and meanings.

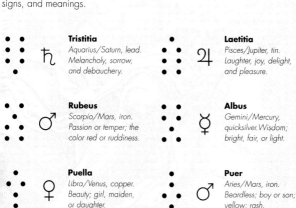

Tristitia
Aquarius/Saturn, lead. Melancholy, sorrow, and debauchery.

Laetitia
Pisces/Jupiter, tin. Laughter, joy, delight, and pleasure.

Rubeus
Scorpio/Mars, iron. Passion or temper; the color red or ruddiness.

Albus
Gemini/Mercury, quicksilver. Wisdom; bright, fair, or light.

Puella
Libra/Venus, copper. Beauty; girl, maiden, or daughter.

Puer
Aries/Mars, iron. Beardless; boy or son; yellow; rash.

Caput Draconis
Northern Node/Jupiter/ Venus, four elements (united). The dragon's head; entrance; upper; ascending.

Cauda Draconis
Southern Node/Saturn, four elements (disunited). The dragon's tail; exit; lower; descending.

The coin throw
Take heads as even and tails as odd and make your 16 throws to get your "mothers."

THE BASIC STEPS
Modern geomancers do not make marks in the earth or sand. Instead, they make random marks on paper with a pencil, toss a coin, cast dice, or draw beans from a bowl—in short, they use any system that will generate a series of 16 random odd and even numbers. Below is the simplest geomantic system devised.

Building the Figure		
THROW	DOTS	BODY PART
1	●	Head
10	● ●	Neck
4	● ●	Body
5	●	Feet

This odd numbered throw represents the feet

The dice throw
The simplest way in which to arrive at your first figures is to throw two dice. An odd number thrown means one dot, and an even number, two dots. Each figure is made up of four throws, the appropriate dots being noted beneath each other in succession as illustrated above.

Mothers and daughters

This throwing process is repeated three more times. Each figure is placed to the left of the previous one. The first four figures are the "four mothers." The last 11 figures are derived from these.

Once you have generated the "four mothers," you can form the "four daughters" as follows. The first "daughter" consists of the "heads" of the "mothers," working from right to left. The second "daughter" is made up of the "necks" of the "mothers," while the third "daughter" is made from the "bodies," and the fourth from the "feet."

HEAD
NECK
BODY
FEET

GEOMANTIC FIGURE

MOTHERS

DAUGHTERS

Building the household

"Mothers" 1 and 2 combine to form "nephew" 1 by adding the two heads, necks, bodies, and feet together, and marking one point if the total is odd and two if it is even. Thus:
"Mothers" 3 and 4 combine to form "nephew" 2.
"Daughters" 1 and 2 combine to form "nephew" 3.
"Daughters" 3 and 4 combine to form "nephew" 4.
"Nephews" 1 and 2 combine to form "witness" 1.
"Nephews" 3 and 4 combine to form "witness" 2.
"Witnesses" 1 and 2 combine to form the "judge."

If the final result is not clear, add the first "mother" to the "judge" to form the "reconciler," which will clarify the result.

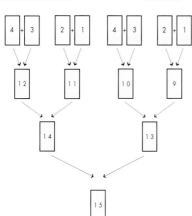

Key	
	Mothers
	Daughters
	Nephews
	Witnesses
	Judge
	Reconciler

Interpreting the Reading

As with many divination methods, geomancy derives a great deal of its potency from its complexity. The procedure of "mothers," "daughters," "nephews," "witnesses," and "judge" concentrates the psychic powers of the reader.

Because of the finality of the last figure, it is also one of the best ways in which to receive a firm "Yes" or "No" answer to a question. The "judge" represents the final answer and the two "witnesses" may be called in to add further meaning to the answer.

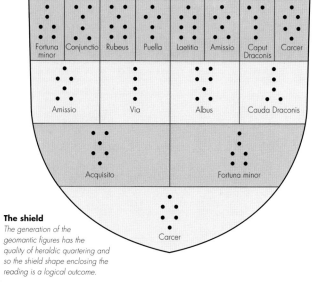

Fortuna minor | Conjunctio | Rubeus | Puella | Laetitia | Amissio | Caput Draconis | Carcer

Amissio | Via | Albus | Cauda Draconis

Acquisito | Fortuna minor

Carcer

The shield

The generation of the geomantic figures has the quality of heraldic quartering and so the shield shape enclosing the reading is a logical outcome.

The question asked in this sample reading was, "Should I remortgage my house to back my new business?"

The "judge" is *Carcer*, indicating restrictions and delays. Although it can also mean prison, in this case it probably represents the extra burden of a larger mortgage.

It doesn't seem promising, but let's look at the witnesses, *Acquisito* and *Fortuna minor*. These are both fairly favorable, in that they show some gains and a little protection. *Fortuna major* would have been a better sign to have as a witness, however.

All in all, the Saturnine quality of *Carcer* indicates that the remortgaging of the house would be too much of an uphill project for the questioner, so we said: "Forget it, it's too risky."

Earth Divination

The word geomancy is derived from the Greek words *Ge*, meaning Gaia or Mother Earth, and *manteia*, meaning "divination."

PALM READING

Since the first prehistoric people decorated their cave walls with handprints, the hand has been of interest to humans. Archaeological digs have unearthed hands made ancient civilizations out of stone, wood, bone, and metal. The use of the thumbprint on documents, as was the practice of ancient Chinese emperors, was the ultimate form of personal signature. ❧ Information on the laws and practice of hand-reading have been found in Indian Vedic texts, while Aristotle (384–322 BC) discovered a text on palm reading on an altar in a temple dedicated to the god Hermes. Greek physicians used palm reading as a clinical aid. Even Julius Caesar (100–44 BC) was said to have judged men's characters using palm reading. ❧ Nowadays, palm reading has become an accepted form of divination. Professional palmists are found in every country in the world, and thousands of books have been written on the subject.

Making a Handprint

The ink

Use a water-based ink to roll the hand. You can get this from most art supply stores. Do not overink your hand.

Making the print

Once the hand is placed on the paper, apply an even pressure on each part of the hand and fingers to make a perfect print.

Storing the prints

Allow the prints to dry completely before handling and keep them in transparent folders for later reference.

The term "palm reading" is somewhat misleading, for a great deal more than the palm of the hand is examined in this type of prediction. By far the best way in which to begin both the study of palm reading and any specific reading is by considering the whole hand. Or, in fact, both hands, since the left hand is said to indicate the potential that one is born with and the right hand reveals the individual nature as it is now, as well as what the future holds in store. (If one is left-handed, then the opposite applies.)

Handprints

There is a great deal to be said for reading someone's hand from a handprint rather than in person. First of all, you can examine the handprint while you are alone, and you should certainly do this in the early stages of learning palm reading anyway. Committing yourself to making pronouncements while you are holding the hand of an excitable client is not conducive to the initial stages of the learning process, and by reading a print you will be in no danger of being

affected by your subject's reaction to your comments. If you store the prints carefully, you will be able to check later whether the hands have changed in any of their details.
If they have, you will be able to ponder what those changes could indicate.

To produce a good print, apply some water-based ink (which is easy to remove later) to a smooth surface, such as a small sheet of glass. Then pass a small roller through it several times. Next, transfer a thin film of ink as evenly as possible to the surfaces of the subject's palm, using the roller. Press the subject's hand carefully, but firmly, onto a sheet of paper (under which there is a soft pad or folded cloth), ensuring that you get a good impression of the center of the palm, as well as the fingers and thumb. Lift the hand from the paper carefully, making sure not to blur the print.

Differences

The differences between the left and right hands can reveal the different directions that the subject has taken during his or her life.

The shape
Much can be learned about a person on first meeting by a simple glance at the hand shape and length and type of fingers.

HAND SHAPES
Before you get involved with the fine details of lines and marks on the palm, you must look at the shape of the entire hand to get a true feeling of someone's character. This will show the basic drive within which all the other factors in the hand will express themselves. It is also an interesting and direct way to gain insight into the character of the people that you meet each day.

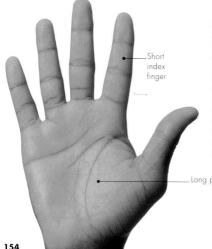

Short index finger

Long palm

Long palm with short fingers
People with this shape of hand relate to the fire signs in astrology. There are always a large number of strong lines in their hands and usually whorl fingerprints. These people tend to be active and outgoing, and are often extroverts. They make excellent leaders and enjoy being in charge and control of other people. Excitable and emotional, their enthusiasm and dash make them a little more vulnerable than most to injuries and accidents.

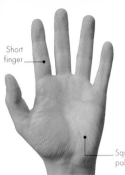

Short finger

Square palm

Square palm with short fingers

People with this shape of hand relate to the earth signs in astrology. There are usually fewer strong lines and often squarer fingertips. These people are rarely comfortable with change. They tend to be slow and steady in their approach and have a strong affinity with nature and the outdoors. They are emotionally stable and make the most reliable workers. Many successful artists and creators have earth-type hands, as do people with trades like carpentry and gardening.

Long finger

Square palm

Square palm with long fingers

This shape relates to the air signs in astrology. Its lines tend to be thin and fingerprints are loops. These people are good at talking, writing, and communication, and often work in the media, publishing, or teaching. They need constant intellectual stimulation.

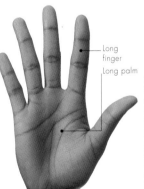

Long finger

Long palm

Long palm with long fingers

People with this shape of hand relate to the water signs in astrology. Their hands tend to have a large number of fine lines and their fingerprints are usually loops. This is the hand of the aesthete, poet, and musician; many of these people will be found working in the fashion and beauty industry, as models and as actresses. Highly sensitive and vulnerable, their emotions are more important to them than reason: their feelings take precedence over logic. Their brilliance often lies in their hunches.

The Fingers

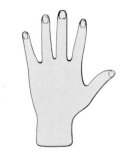

Long, medium, or short?
The length of the fingers provides fascinating and revealing insights into a person's nature.

Close observation of an individual's fingers, thumbs, and fingertips will give you clues to their character.

The index finger

Long: self-confidence and awareness; able and ambitious, a leader type; indispensable during a crisis.
Medium: reveals a healthy balance between confidence and modesty.
Short: indicates shyness, fear of failure, insecurity, and self-doubt.

The middle finger

Long: highly ambitious, with little humor; works hard to get ahead.
Medium: reveals a good sense of when to work and when to play; mature behavior.
Short: careless and disorganized in working patterns; dislikes routine.

The ring finger

Long: shows a creative nature, indicates ability in art or fashion design; can reveal a gambling nature.
Medium: modestly creative, but in a conservative, traditional way.
Short: indicates little creativity.

The little finger

Long: indicates high intelligence; these people make good writers and speakers, and have a stronger than average sex drive.
Medium: indicative of the "happy medium": not too bright and not too dim.
Short: shows emotional immaturity, gullibility, susceptibility, and naïveté.

Fingertip shapes

Square: careful, rational, methodical thinkers who tend to lack creativity.

Pointed: sensitive, fragile people; often artists, writers, poets, and daydreamers.

Conic: flexible dispositions, with the ability to negotiate; emotional security is important to them.

Spatulate: people who take action; usually dynamic thinkers, inventors, explorers, and innovators.

Fingernails

Square: easy-going, even temperament.

Broad: strong character with an explosive temper.

Fan-shaped: indicates long-term stress.

Almond: a gentle and kind daydreamer.

Narrow: a cold and selfish personality.

Vertical ridges: the subject may suffer from rheumatic problems.

Horizontal ridges: the subject may have dietary deficiencies.

Dished: the subject may be suffering from a chemical imbalance.

Wedge-shaped: an oversensitive, touchy character.

The thumb

The thumb reveals a person's drive and how it is applied. Of the two phalanges, or bones, the top phalange denotes willpower and the bottom phalange indicates how far the person will push in order to achieve their desires.

Large: a strong personality.

Small: a lack of energy and willpower.

Long and broad: a character who pushes hard to succeed.

Long and narrow: a person who needs to succeed, but rarely has the necessary driving force.

Short and thick: an obstinate nature.

Flexible: an easy-going, generous, and tolerant person.

Straight and stiff: a reliable, reserved, cautious, and stubborn character.

Close to the side of the hand: a miserly person.

Sticking out widely: a happy-go-lucky personality.

THE MAJOR LINES

The life line does not indicate how long you will live; it shows the quality of your life and how much strength and energy you have. The heart line reveals your basic emotional character, needs, and drives. (Interestingly, partners in successful marriages often have similar heart lines.) The head line indicates the way you think, but not necessarily your intelligence level. The fate line indicates your direction or aim in life.

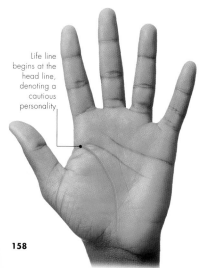

Life line
begins at the
head line,
denoting a
cautious
personality

The life line

A life line that starts close to the thumb denotes a person of low vitality.

A life line that makes a wide curve shows a person who has plenty of vitality.

When the life line is less strongly marked than the head line, it reveals a person who is mentally, rather than physically, driven.

A life line that has a chained appearance indicates delicate health.

Small lines rising from the life line denote an active and versatile personality.

Lines swinging out from the life line indicate a love of travel.

Small lines leading from the life line refer to particular events at specific times of life.

The heart line

A strongly curved heart line denotes a person who is demonstrative in love and takes the lead in relationships.

A straight heart line suggests a more passive and receptive emotional character.

A heart line that develops a steep curve below the index and middle fingers indicates someone who has strong sexual desires.

When the heart line ends under the middle finger, the subject requires constant reassurance and love

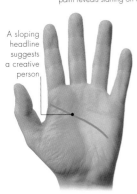

The fate line

A strong fate line indicates a person who has settled into a steady pattern of life.

A weak fate line denotes someone who is unsettled and changes jobs frequently.

A fate line beginning at the bottom of the palm reveals starting on a life path early.

A sloping headline suggests a creative person

If the fate line extends almost to the middle finger, the subject will probably remain active well into old age

The head line

A long head line indicates a person who thinks things through slowly and carefully.

A short head line denotes someone whose thinking is quick, incisive, and to the point.

A straight head line reveals clear, concentrated thinking.

A curved head line indicates a person who thinks laterally and toys with new ideas.

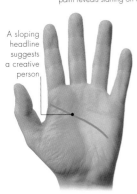

The Minor Lines

As well as the four major lines, there are other lines and influence marks found on the hand that hold special significance.

The Mars line

The Mars line runs inside the life line and indicates extra vitality, as well as a form of secondary protection and backup to the life line.

The via lascivia

The via lascivia is a horizontal line running across the mount of the Moon (see page 162). In past times it was thought to represent lewd and promiscuous behavior, but nowadays it is linked to addiction of some kind. It is also known as the allergy line and can indicate a person's general sensitivity to allergens.

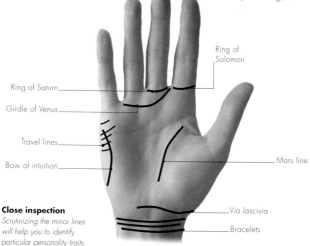

Ring of Solomon

Ring of Saturn

Girdle of Venus

Travel lines

Bow of intuition

Mars line

Via lascivia

Bracelets

Close inspection

Scrutinizing the minor lines will help you to identify particular personality traits.

Travel lines

Travel lines are horizontal lines that enter the palm from the percussion edge (the outer side of the hand below the little finger). They lie across the mount of the Moon in the bottom left corner and the Mars lower mount on the outside edge of the palm beneath the mount of Mercury under the little finger. The longer and stronger each line, the more important the journey.

The bracelets

The bracelets are the rings between the palm and wrist. A top bracelet that is curved and pushed up toward the palm indicates that there may be a weakness in the reproductive area. Three strong bracelets are said to indicate a long life.

The girdle of Venus

This rare marking is a semicircular pattern above the heart line that covers the two middle mounts. Often faint and fragmented, it indicates a person who is highly sensitive.

The bow of intuition

This is another unusual marking. Found on the percussion side of the palm, starting on the mount of the Moon and curving around below the mount of Mercury finger, it usually indicates someone who has extraordinary intuitive abilities, who may even exhibit clairvoyance and the gift of prophecy.

The ring of Saturn

This rare line is a small arc under the middle finger. Enclosing the Saturn mount, it suggests someone who is reclusive and withdrawn, perhaps even miserly.

The ring of Solomon

The ring of Solomon skirts the mount of Jupiter. It is usually found in the hands of people who have a great deal of common sense. Those who have a pronounced version of this mark will often make good lawyers, judges, politicians, and teachers.

Planets

The planetary correspondences, as in astrology, represent certain drives and emphases that the character may have, depending on their prominence.

THE MOUNTS

The mounts are the raised portions of the palm, which vary from hand to hand. Some are more pronounced than others, even on the same hand, and this tells us about the character of the person who has them. To decide whether a mount is large, well developed, or lean, you will have to compare it to the hand's other mounts.

◯ The mount of Venus
This is found at the base of the thumb.
Broad and firmly developed: a strong sex drive.
High and soft: excitable and fickle.
Underdeveloped or flat: a delicate constitution or poor health.

◯ The mount of the Moon
This is found in the bottom corner of the hand, under the Mars lower.
Normal size: sensitivity and perceptiveness.
Very large: a vivid imagination, introspection, and possibly untruthfulness.
Flat: unimaginative, unstable, and cold.

◯ The mount of Jupiter
This is the mound at the base of the index finger.
Well rounded: confident.
Large: generous.
Extra high: bossy.
Flat: selfish, lazy, and inconsiderate.

◯ The mount of Saturn
This rises under the middle finger.
Large: a gloomy, almost reclusive, attitude.
Flat or undeveloped: a lackluster, unimaginative person.
Merging with Jupiter: an ambitious, serious person who aims high.
Merging with Mercury: an intense lover of the arts.

The mount of the Sun (Apollo)

This is found at the base of the ring finger.

Normal size: a person of sunny disposition, good taste, and artistic leanings.

Large: hedonistic, extravagant, and pretentious.

Flat: dull, aimless, and uninterested in culture.

The mount of Mercury

This is found at the base of the little finger.

Large: a good sense of humor and a warm, receptive nature.

Normal: a quick-thinking, subtle, and persuasive person.

Flat: dull, unimaginative, gullible, and a loner.

Mars upper

The Mars upper is tucked into the crease of the thumb.

Large: a bad-tempered, sarcastic, and cruel person.

Normal: morally courageous.

Flat: a cowardly, self-preserving person.

Mars lower

The Mars lower is found on the outside edge of the hand, between Mercury and the Moon.

Large: violent and argumentative.

Normal: courageous and a fighter.

Flat: cowardly.

The mount of Neptune

This sits in the middle of the hand, at the base of the palm. Although it is not often prominent, if it is well developed it indicates a charismatic person.

SECRETS OF DIVINATION

Special Marks

Minor marks

Because these are usually small and difficult for a novice to see, a powerful magnifying glass is an important tool.

These minor marks demonstrate the importance of doing your readings from handprints, because the tiny lines will show up more clearly than when looking at the hand alone.

Stars

The star is the hand's most highly favored indication of good fortune. It is, however, only potent when found on the mounts of Jupiter, Mercury, and the Sun, as well as at any point along the Sun line (a sister line to the fate line, which can start anywhere and reaches toward the middle finger) and at the top of the fate line. If a star is on the Jupiter mount, it indicates good fortune, marriage into money, and a position of importance in life. On the Sun mount, it indicates talents that will bring fame and fortune (stars in this position are often seen on the hands of successful actors). A star found on the Apollo line indicates a major money win.

Crosses

Unlike the star, the cross is not usually a good indication. As with all lines, the less distinct it is, the less powerful it will be. On the mount of the Sun, a cross suggests disappointment in money matters or business. On the mount of Mercury, it denotes a dishonest nature. On the mount of Venus, it indicates a negative influence on relationships or affections. On the mount of the Moon, it shows a propensity toward self-deception. A clear cross on the mount of Saturn is particularly malefic and warns of setbacks to life ambitions.

Forked lines

Forked lines show diversity, or a scattering of interests, related to the meaning of the particular line. On the life line, they can suggest changes of direction in life. On the heart line, they reveal changeable, or split, affections, and perhaps love affairs. A fork at the end of the head line denotes an individual with good business acumen. On the fate line, particularly at the end, a fork can indicate a successful career, or fame and fortune.

Islands

Islands found on any line indicate weaknesses, lack of energy, and periods of stress, and even breakdowns. On the heart lines they can denote hearing or sight problems.

Ascending lines

Smaller lines branching upward from the main lines of the hand indicate increased energy. If they continue toward any of the mounts, the mount in question indicates the realm of energy to which they refer.

Descending lines

Smaller lines branching downward from a main line indicate a lessening of energy and interest in matters governed by the main line from which they descend.

Grilles

Grilles often occur on the mounts. They denote obstacles and even a lack of success in whatever that particular mount is associated with.

Minor Marks

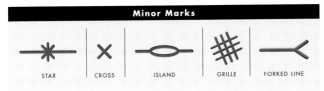

STAR | CROSS | ISLAND | GRILLE | FORKED LINE

TASSEOGRAPHY

Tasseography is a grand name for the art of reading tealeaves. Although most people use teabags nowadays, this change of preference need not deter you from practicing perhaps the most homespun of all of the methods of divination. In common with many divination methods, the origins of tasseography (*tasse* is the French word for cup) seem to have been Chinese, having developed from the Chinese method of divination based on reading and interpreting the appearance of the insides of bells. When they were turned over, the handleless Chinese teacups not only resembled bells, but were also more easy to transport.

Preparing for a Reading

Placing the cup
The timescale and intensity of the symbols are based on their position in the cup. The handle faces the questioner.

Tasseography has been a favorite form of divination for people in the British Isles for centuries, perhaps because of the popularity of tea there. Quite simply, it was convenient to use tea leaves in order to bring out of oneself an awareness or "knowing" that ordinary, mundane activities would not normally allow. This was particularly the case where the long winters and rainy days encouraged greater introspection. Some people maintain stronger contact with this level of so-called psychicism or intuition.

If you live in a household in which coffee is the staple drink, then use coffee grains by all means. Whether you are using tea or coffee, however, it is necessary to make the brew in the traditional way: tea in a teapot and coffee in a jug. With tea, the best results are achieved when using not too fine a leaf, and you must not use a strainer. Although many Chinese teas have larger leaves that produce little dust and result in more direct images, a mixture of your own making could be the best solution. The same applies to coffee grains, which should be medium ground and not filtered. Allow the grains to fall to the bottom of the jug before the coffee is poured.

Doing a reading

It is important that whoever is asking the question should drink the tea. When there is just a little liquid left, the cup should be quickly rotated clockwise to swirl the leaves around and the liquid almost allowed to reach the top of the cup. When you are satisfied that the leaves have been well distributed, invert the cup on the saucer, allowing the remaining tea to drain away. Turn the cup over so that the handle faces the questioner and commence the reading.

The handle represents the questioner, and all judgements of time are based on his or her position in relation to the handle. Images near the top of the cup are close in time, while images near the bottom are distant. Images to the right of the handle are in the future, while those to the left are in the past. The further away from the handle the images are, the more distant in time they are. The flat disk of the cup's bottom is usually thought to be a less fortunate area.

How you interpret the images is entirely up to you.

Choosing a Cup

It is worth searching for a cup of the best design for tasseography. It should be wide at the mouth, with sloping sides and a smooth, plain, white inner surface.

HEART

HORSESHOE

SNAKE

THE SYMBOLS

Descriptions and meanings attributed to tasseography symbols are always very basic. It is only through much practice that one becomes able to build individual interpretations into a complete story involving the past and future of the questioner. If the cup shows no positive images, then you must be bold and discontinue the reading. It is pointless to invent images that have not strongly imposed themselves on your mind. A lack of imagery is a message that you should proceed no further on this occasion.

Preparing the cup

Whoever is asking the question should drink the tea, leaving a small amount in the bottom of the cup. The reader then swirls the liquid around the cup in a clockwise motion to ensure an even distribution of the tea leaves.

Draining the tea

The cup is then turned upside down on the saucer so that the liquid can drain away. The reader turns the cup over, making sure the handle faces the questioner, and proceeds to interpret the tea-leaf patterns.

Individual

Each of the symbols to the right could be seen as something else. What you, the reader, see is the important thing.

DAGGER   BROOM   ANCHOR

The positions

For a clear reading, the cup should have a wide rim, sloping sides, and a white inner surface. Patterns that form at the top of the cup are close in time, while those at the bottom of the cup are more distant. Images to the right of the handle represent the future and images to the left represent the past.

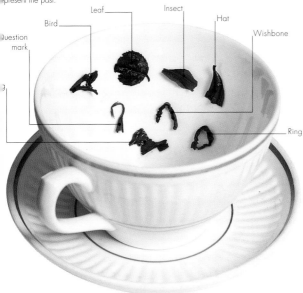

Question mark

Bird

Leaf

Insect

Hat

Wishbone

Ring

Symbols and
Their Meanings

A

Acorn: top of cup: financial success; middle of cup: good health; bottom of cup: improvement in health or finances.
Airplane: a sudden journey; a disappointment.
Anchor: top of cup: success in business and romance; middle of cup: a prosperous voyage; bottom of cup: social success.
Apple: a business achievement.
Arrow: unpleasant news.
Ax: difficulties overcome.

B

Bag: a trap.
Ball: a person connected with sport; changeable fortunes.
Balloon: short-term troubles.
Bird: good news.
Boat: a visit from a friend; a safe refuge.
Book, open: legal actions or future success; closed: delay or difficult studies.
Boot: achievement; protection; pointing away from handle: dismissal; broken: failure.
Bottle, one bottle: pleasure; several bottles: illness.
Box, open: romantic troubles solved; closed: the lost will be found.
Branch, with leaves: a birth; without leaves: a disappointment.
Bridge: opportunity for success.
Building: a house move.
Bull: prosperity; good health.
Butterfly: a carefree attitude.

C

Candle: help, knowledge.
Car: fortunate journey.
Castle: financial gain through marriage; high position.
Cat: a quarrel; danger.
Chain, unbroken: a wedding; broken: a termination.
Chair: unexpected extra guest.
Cherries: a win.
Church: marriage or birth.
Circle: success; a wedding.
Clouds: trouble ahead.
Clover: prosperity.
Coin: monetary gain.
Crescent: start of a journey.
Cross: a sacrifice; difficulties.
Crown: recognition; success; a wish coming true; a legacy.
Cup: reward; a secret.

D

Dagger: impetuosity; a sudden shock; enemies plotting.
Dog: faithful friendship.
Door: a new beginning.
Dots: add emphasis to the meaning of any nearby symbol.
Drum: scandal; gossip.

E

Ear: malicious rumors.
Egg: a new project; prosperity.
Elephant: wisdom; strength; success; a trustworthy friend.
Envelope: good news.

F

Face, smiling: happiness; grimacing: opposition.
Fan: flirtation; indiscretion.
Feather: instability; inconstancy.
Feet: an important decision.
Fence: limits; overprotectiveness.
Finger: emphasizes the symbol to which it points.
Fish: good fortune in all things.
Flower: a small kindness.
Fly: domestic irritations.
Fork: a false friend; flattery.
Forked line: decisions.
Fountain: future success.
Fruit: prosperity.

G

Gallows: financial, social loss.
Gate: future happiness.
Grapes: prosperity.

H

Hand: a new friendship.
Hat: a new job; a change.
Head: new opportunities; a position of responsibility.
Heart: love and marriage.

Hill: an obstacle ahead.
Horn: abundance.
Horse: sincerity; galloping: good news; head only: romance.
Horseshoe: good luck.
House: security.

Initials: represent people known.
Insect: minor problems.

Jewelry: a welcome gift.
Jug: good health.

Kettle, near handle of cup: domestic bliss; near or at bottom of cup: domestic strife.
Key: new opportunities; two keys near bottom of cup: robbery.
Kite: lofty aspirations.
Knife: broken relationships; near handle of cup: divorce; bottom of cup: lawsuits.

Ladder: advancement.
Leaf: prosperity; good fortune.
Lines, straight: progress or journeys; wavy: uncertainty or disappointment; slanting: business failure.

Man: a visitor; arm outstretched: bringing gifts.
Moon, full: a love affair; first quarter: new projects; last quarter: declining fortunes; obscured: depression; surrounded by dots: marriage for money.
Mountain: high ambition.

Nail: malice; injustice; pain.
Numbers: a timescale or the number of days before an event.

Octopus: danger.
Owl: gossip; scandal; failure.

Palm tree: success; honor.
Pipe: thoughts; solution.
Pistol: danger; unpleasant persuasion.

Question mark: hesitancy; caution.

Ring: top: marriage; middle: proposal; bottom: long engagement; complete: happy marriage; broken with a cross next to it: broken engagement.

Scales: balanced: justice; unbalanced: injustice.
Scissors: unhappiness through domestic arguments; separation.
Shell: good news.
Ship: a successful journey.
Snake: an enemy.
Spider: persistence; secrecy; future money.
Spoon: generosity.
Star: health, happiness; five-pointed star: good fortune; eight-pointed star: accidents or reverses; five stars: success without happiness; seven stars: grief.

Steps: an improvement.
Sun: success; power.
Sword: disputes or quarrels.

Table: social gathering.
Teapot: a committee meeting.
Tent: an unsettled life; a love of adventure.
Tree: prosperity; ambitions fulfilled; surrounded by dots: fortune in the country.
Triangle: unexpected; pointing upward: success; pointing downward: failure.
Trident: success at sea.

Umbrella: annoyance; a need for shelter; if open: shelter found; if shut: shelter refused.

Vase: a friend in need.

Walking stick: a visitor.
Waterfall: prosperity.
Whale: business success.
Wheel: complete: good fortune; broken: disappointment; near rim: unexpected money.
Window: open: good luck; closed: disappointment.
Wings: messages.
Wishbone: a wish granted.
Woman: pleasure.

Yacht: pleasure.

DICE AND DOMINOES

Stones, wooden cubes, bones, sticks, and shells marked with a series of dots have all been used as different forms of games from time immemorial. It is natural that these in turn should have developed into simple methods of foretelling the future. One cast and the truth is told. ⟐ There is a compulsive quality about the little dice cubes, or die, as they are called individually. This was expressed in the 1970s' bestselling book *The Dice Man*, by Luke Rhinehart, which told the story of a bored psychiatrist who chose to decide each event in his life with a throw of the dice.

Dice

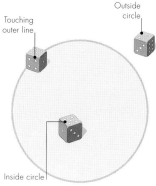

Touching outer line

Outside circle

Inside circle

Throwing the dice
Three dice are thrown into a circle. As well as the number, where they land can also affect the reading.

There are many ways of doing a dice reading, but the one that has become the standard is the circle method. Draw a circle with a diameter of roughly 12 inches (around 30 centimeters) on a large piece of card, and reserve it to use as your diceboard. Three dice cubes are then thrown onto this board in order to create the divination reading. If a die lands outside the circle, or if it touches the outer line, it is ignored.

Doing a reading

Whatever the meanings of the dice inside the circle, they will be adversely affected by any dice that are outside the circle. If only one lands inside the circle and its number is less than three, throw it again. If none lands inside the circle, throw them again as well. If, after a rethrow, all of the dice have landed outside the circle, the time is unpropitious, so abandon the reading.

The meaning of the throws

These are the meanings of the various dice throws.

Three: a favorable throw, signifying good luck with your wishes.

Four: disappointment is close at hand.

Five: your wish will come true; a stranger will bring you much happiness.

Six: losses in business or material matters, but gains in spiritual life.

Seven: unfounded accusations are made against you; malicious gossip.

Eight: be prepared to make changes; the course you are pursuing is not going to succeed.

Nine: good for love affairs; quarrels will end in reconciliation.

Ten: family happiness; good fortune in business and financial matters.

Eleven: a parting from someone close.

Twelve: some correspondence will require a quick decision; ask for a friend's advice.

Thirteen: sorrow or regrets that will last for a long time.

Fourteen: a new friend will enter your life and will become very dear to you.

Fifteen: beware of involvement in a dishonest or dubious scheme.

Sixteen: a good omen for a future journey that will be of great benefit.

Seventeen: a stranger from abroad will offer valuable advice.

Eighteen: the best of all dice omens, indicating success, happiness, or promotion very soon.

Stormy Weather

It is traditional to refrain from doing dice readings on Mondays, or on days when the weather is stormy, since the readings will be erratic and inaccurate at those times.

The tiles

As with other forms of divination, the better the tools, the more special the reading becomes. Look for an old set of dominoes and if you're lucky it will have a fine wooden box that will add to the feeling of the ritual.

DOMINOES
Dice and dominoes are everyday objects, but they should be stored carefully if you are using them for divination. Keeping them in a box or cloth reserved for them, in a secret place that no others will invade, will give them a special quality. Remember that the more respectfully you treat your divination tools, the greater the rapport you will develop with them, thus enhancing the information they can impart.

Doing a reading

Before doing the reading, the 28 domino tiles are shuffled face down, as in any domino game. Three dominoes are taken from the selection, one at a time, as the reading is done. Ask a specific question, and, if possible, relate the answers to that question only.

Jane's sister Valerie became engaged three months ago and was about to move in with her fiancé. Despite this happy event, Jane knew her sister felt insecure about this because a previous engagement had been broken off soon after the couple had moved in together. Jane decided to do a reading to ask the dominoes whether her sister's current relationship would be successful.

The following dominoes were chosen:

Four-three fears about problems or disappointments will be unfounded.
Six-one an end to your problems in which a good friend could be involved; a wedding is in the offing.
Five-two the birth of a child to someone in the family.

Fortune
Many of the dominoes can foretell good luck and fortune (or even misfortune) where money is concerned.

A newborn
Pick a five-two domino and this may predict a baby on the way.

Interpreting the Dominoes

Once you have asked your question and selected the three dominoes for your reading, consult the table below for the interpretations related to them.

Remember that you need to ask the dominoes a specific question. It is important not to make more than one consultation in a day, since this will trivialize the system.

 Six-six: the best domino, with strong omens for success and happiness in all areas of life.

 Six-five: patience and perseverance are indicated; a kind action will bring you satisfaction.

 Six-four: arguments, or maybe even a lawsuit, with an unsuccessful outcome.

 Six-three: an important journey that will affect your life; a happy vacation.

 Six-two: good luck is coming your way soon; circumstances will change for the better.

 Six-one: an end to your problems in which a good friend could be involved; a wedding is in the offing.

 Six-blank: guard against false friends or a deceitful person; someone does not wish you well.

 Five-five: a change will bring success; a move to a new place will make you happy.

 Five-four: material profits and good fortune through wise forethought (but do not speculate with the profit).

 Five-three: an important visit from someone who can help you.

 Five-two: the birth of a child to someone in the family.

 Five-one: a passionate love affair, or an exciting meeting with a new friend, in the near future, which may not end happily.

 Five-blank: you may have to comfort a friend in trouble, but be cautious and carefully consider how to help.

 Four-four: happiness, fun, and celebration—perhaps a party.

Four-three: fears about problems or disappointments will be unfounded.

 Four-two: beware of someone in your group who is deceitful and a cheat.

 Four-one: financial problems lie ahead; make sure that you pay any outstanding debts.

 Four-blank: someone whom you have slighted will reappear on the scene; try to reconcile the quarrel.

 Three-three: there are obstacles, like jealousy or distress, in your love life; money matters look more favorable.

 Three-two: not a good time for taking financial risks of any kind; avoid anything that suggests a gamble.

 Three-one: some surprising news could prove useful, but beware of problems caused by new acquaintances.

 Three-blank: this domino is not a good omen, and suggests unexpected problems through jealousy.

 Two-two: a happy marriage of great importance is indicated, even if it is not your own.

 Two-one: although loss of money or property is indicated, this domino is a good omen in relation to your social life and old friends.

 Two-blank: a good omen for travel and meeting new friends who will become dear to you.

 One-one: a time for brave and bold decisions that will improve your life.

 One-blank: a stranger or outsider will bring some interesting news that will prove of great help in your life.

 Blank-blank: this is the worst domino in the set and carries the worst omens; the double blank can have a negative effect on all of your activities.

SCRYING

The crystal ball is probably the most familiar symbol of the world of fortune-telling and divination. Rarely will a television documentary on astrology, psychics, or the occult be screened without moody shots of a shrouded figure gazing into a candlelit crystal ball. ❧ Scrying is the art of divination by gazing deeply into a reflective surface. The fact that many people see potent images while looking into the still waters of a lake, or gazing at the flickering flames of a fire, probably has something to do with how this oracle originally developed. ❧ Scrying has been with us for centuries and was originally linked with hydromancy because water was the first medium to be used as a reflective device. The Babylonians used sacred bowls filled with liquid, while the Egyptians held a pool of ink in their cupped hands for scrying.

How to Choose a Crystal

The crystal

Only your hands should ever touch the crystal. If anyone else touches it you should repeat your initial preparation and cleansing before any further use.

Nowadays, the most popular instrument used for scrying is the crystal ball. This form of divination is known as crystallomancy.

Unlike cards, dice, dominoes, the tarot, reading tealeaves, and other forms of divination, scrying is not a matter of dealing out a random selection of images and then interpreting them. It is a much deeper art, which entails tapping into your inner visualization abilities. At the root of all forms of divination is the need for the diviner to have a perfectly developed inner perceptiveness that enables the translation of visual images into positive and meaningful predictions. It is not unlike the way in which a truly creative artist brings a sculpture or painting to life, or a psychologist diagnoses a condition or pattern after a patient offers a series of clues.

Your "inner crystal"

Successful crystallomancy is not simply a matter of buying an expensive crystal ball and then looking hard into it hoping to see images—you won't see a thing. You must find the perfect crystal for you, one that relates to your inner self. This ideal match is at the root of successful scrying. Your "inner crystal" can only be found through meditation and developing your potential ability to achieve altered states.

The crystal that speaks to you may be one of several kinds. The most usual is a beryl or quartz sphere, about 4 inches (about 10 centimeters) in diameter. If you choose to use a glass ball instead, you should examine it carefully first to make sure that it is free of any blemishes or bubbles that could distract you.

To prepare your crystal ball, wash it in a thin solution of vinegar and water and polish it with a soft cloth. Keep it wrapped in a cloth when not in use, and let no one else handle it. Do not allow direct sunlight to fall on it, as this is believed to ruin the sensitivity of the crystal. Moonlight, however, is said to be beneficial, and some scryers even take their crystals out for a moonbathe when there is a full moon.

Ancient Tradition

The Mayans, Incas, Native Americans, and Australian aborigines used similar methods for scrying, and it is known that crystal balls were used in Europe from the fifth century AD.

PRACTICING WITH THE CRYSTAL

Before you begin, remember that most people generally see nothing on the first or subsequent sittings, so don't worry if you don't see anything during your initial attempts at scrying. There is a road to crystal vision, but it is only open to those who are calm, patient, and persistent.

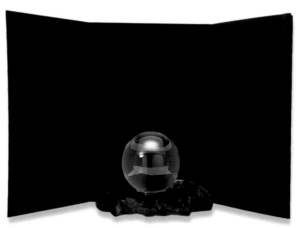

Preparation and reading

Take your crystal to a quiet room where you will not be disturbed. The lighting conditions in the room should resemble the light on a cloudy or wet day. Place your crystal on a stand, or a black velvet cushion, on a table and partially surround it with a black velvet curtain or screen.

The presence of any other person will initially be a handicap to your concentration and should therefore be avoided. When you have developed your powers, questions may asked by other people, but only in a very low voice. Sit comfortably and fix your eyes on the crystal with a steady, calm gaze. On the first occasion, do this for ten minutes only (place a watch so that you can see its face, but not hear it ticking). The next seven sittings can last up to 15 minutes, and although you can gradually increase the length of your sessions after that, never exceed one hour.

Crystal visions

When the crystal begins to look dull or cloudy, with small points of light glittering in it like tiny stars, you are beginning to gain crystalline vision. In time, this cloudy appearance will quite suddenly give way to a blue ocean of space, against which the vision will be clearly apparent.

Two main kinds of vision typically show themselves to the sitter: first, symbolic visions, indicated by the appearance of such symbols as a boat, tree, bird, and so on; and, second, scenes and people. In the case of symbolic visions, much will depend on the ability of the scryer to translate them. They generally have similar meanings to those outlined in the tasseography section of this book (see pages 172–73).

Timing

Regarding the timing of any events seen, as a general rule, visions that appear in the extreme background indicate a more distant time— in either the past or the future— than those observed nearer at hand, while those that appear in the foreground denote either the present or the immediate future.

The images

Allow images to come and go. Do not try to hold on to them so that more flow into your awareness. Remain relaxed and do not attempt to control the crystal visions.

187

Famous Scryers

John Dee
Diviner and alchemist John Dee practiced scrying and astrology at the court of Queen Elizabeth I of England.

Thousands of records of predictions and warnings given by various divining methods have been recorded throughout history, but the number of cases in which we are certain that scrying was used are quite few and far between. Two notable prophets who used the mirror and the crystal for scrying were the well-known seer Nostradamus (1503–66) and the astrologer and diviner, Dr. John Dee (1527–1608). It is probably not a coincidence that these scryers were contemporaries.

Nostradamus

Probably one of the most famous seers in history, Nostradamus is known for his *Centuries*, a body of poetic prophesies covering the centuries beyond his own time. He is still the subject of many hundreds of books, even today. He described his method of divining as looking into a dish of water placed upon a tripod. Although Nostradamus also used astrology, most of his predictions were produced through scrying.

He had many other talents. As a physician he specialized in curing victims of the plague, and soon became recognized as one of the foremost experts on healing people of it. Somewhat surprisingly, he was also an excellent jam-maker, and he made perfumes, which were in great demand among the ladies of the French court. He predicted his own death to the actual day, and even the date when looters would threaten his grave, on which he had engraved his prediction. Needless to say, it was left alone.

Dr. John Dee

An astrologer and diviner, Dr. Dee cast an astrological chart for Queen Elizabeth I of England when she came to the throne in 1558. He used a shiny black obsidian mirror, or "show stone," for scrying, which was said to have come from the Aztecs or Mayans. (It is now in the British Museum, London, along with his conjuring table, which contains the Enochian alphabet that he used as an "angel language.") He performed many of his prophesying tasks with the psychic Edward Kelley (who was known for being a rebel, which got him into trouble with an enemy of Queen Elizabeth and led to his imprisonment) and was also an alchemist, cabbalist, and an adept in esoteric and occult lore.

Like Nostradamus, Dr. Dee was extremely versatile, doing much work on the development of navigation. He became a spy for the queen, and was renowned for having the largest library in England at that time, which consisted of over 4,000 books.

CLAIRVOYANCE

Clairvoyance is the psychic ability to know, or become aware of, something without the help of any outside influences, and is often called "the sixth sense." Hunches, *déjà vu* moments, and strange feelings that all is not well are classed as types of clairvoyance. We make inexplicable decisions about people that are not based on logical or practical information and we get feelings about houses that are "spooky," places that feel "loved and lived in." Many clairvoyants use trance methods to produce their clear visions, while others hear voices or "see" events as visions. A notable outcome of the growing interest in psychic phenomena was the development of Zener cards during the 1880s. These cards, which may picture a square, circle, star, cross, or wavy lines, are picked at random from a shuffled deck after the person being tested has made his or her prediction. Making or buying a deck of such "ESP" (extra-sensory perception) cards may prove an easy way to test your clairvoyance.

Psychometry

Peter Hurkos
Peter Hurkos was a consultant to police chiefs around the world and to every American president from Eisenhower to Reagan.

Psychometry is the ability to reveal information through contact with objects belonging to, or used by, persons unknown to the psychic. The theory is that whenever anyone touches an object, sympathetic vibrations become attached to it that can be relived, or read, by psychics.

Peter Hurkos's "gift"

A psychic's ability to pick up information from objects whose owner is absent has led to their use by the police for the purpose of finding missing persons. A notable example was the Dutchman Peter Hurkos (1911–88), who gained his psychic gift after falling from a ladder and suffering a serious brain injury. Having been in a coma for three days, he discovered on regaining consciousness that he had developed an ability to see the past, present, and future, particularly when holding objects belonging to other people.

In 1956, Hurkos was brought to the USA for tests at a medical research laboratory. He underwent tests for two-and-a-half years under very tightly controlled conditions. The results convinced Dr. Puharich, the doctor who was conducting the tests, that Hurkos's psychic abilities were provable with an astonishing accuracy rate of 90 per cent.

Hurkos's reputation spread, and, after settling in the USA, he worked with the police as a psychic detective on many famous cases. Among other things, he assisted police in their searches for the "Boston Strangler" and the murderers of Sharon Tate. He received countless police badges from police chiefs around the world, including one from the International Criminal Police Organization. Perhaps surprisingly, Hurkos's gift was accepted by the Roman Catholic church. He was even decorated by Pope Pius XII, who reportedly said, "I hope you will always use your God-given gift for the betterment of mankind."

It seems that psychometry is indeed a gift, and, although it can be improved with practice, it is not something that can be taught from scratch. Of course, if you never hold a given object to your forehead and try to tune in to the vibrations and emanations it may give out, you will never know if you have psychometric abilities.

Psychic Conductors

Metal objects, such as jewelry, seem to be the most powerful conductors of psychometric energy, and the more they have been handled, the more information they impart.

Virgil

Our piece of Virgil's Aenid picked at random was: "So winds, when yet unfledg'd in woods they lie, In whispers first their tender voices try." Is this a reminder to approach your talents with care and not to run before you can walk?

CLAIRVOYANT DEVICES

The controversial Ouija board is said to help people make contact with "spirits," who may be good or evil. Most people, however, believe that it is just another way of tapping into the questioner's subconscious. Automatic writing relies on the uncontrolled response of the questioner's hand to divine an answer to a question. Practicing bibliomancy involves closing the eyes, opening a book, and then pointing to a word on the questioner's page—the word chosen is said to reveal the answer to the question.

Ouija boards

These vary from improvised handwritten letters on paper squares to the elaborate and decorative board illustrated here. This also shows planetary symbols.

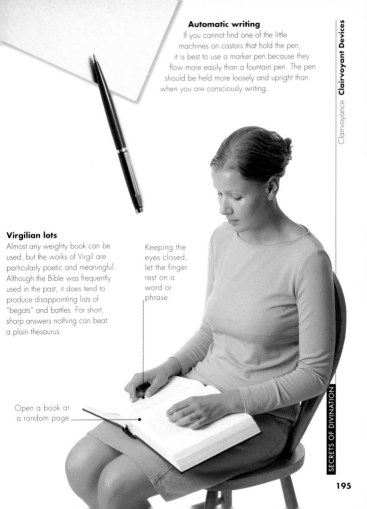

Automatic writing

If you cannot find one of the little
machines on castors that hold the pen,
it is best to use a marker pen because they
flow more easily than a fountain pen. The pen
should be held more loosely and upright than
when you are consciously writing.

Virgilian lots

Almost any weighty book can be
used, but the works of Virgil are
particularly poetic and meaningful.
Although the Bible was frequently
used in the past, it does tend to
produce disappointing lists of
"begats" and battles. For short,
sharp answers nothing can beat
a plain thesaurus.

Keeping the
eyes closed,
let the finger
rest on a
word or
phrase

Open a book at
a random page

How the Devices Work

Bibliomancy
*If you don't have shelves and shelves
of books yourself, try the public library
for the book by row, shelf, book,
page, and line method.*

These three clairvoyance techniques have a long history. Although charlatans have a field day with such methods, they do sometimes seem to work with remarkable accuracy.

The Ouija board

A small, wheeled device holding a pointer is placed on a board marked with the letters of the alphabet, and often also with the words "Yes" and "No." The fingertips of one or more people are placed on the device and a question is asked. The letters to which the pointer slides are noted and later translated. If the reading is satisfactory, the question will have been answered.

The first commercial Ouija board was produced in Baltimore in 1892 by a cabinetmaker named William Flud. It became immensely popular with the spiritualist groups that were prolific at that time. The rights to the original board were bought by the toymakers Parker Brothers, and hundreds of thousands of them are still produced.

Automatic writing

A wheeled device similar to that of the Ouija board, but with the addition of a penholder, is used. The device is arranged on a sheet of paper and the fingers are placed on a small platform. The questioner meditates on the question, and, as the hand inadvertently moves, the pen makes continuous marks on the paper. When the person feels that the answer is complete, the writing is examined for any word, or even sentence, that may have appeared.

Automatic writing can also be performed by holding a pen to paper, closing the eyes, and allowing the pen to wander at will. It is rare that one will have unconsciously written neat and legible words, but, as with all forms of divination, it is on the interpretation of the final result that the success or failure of the experiment depends.

Bibliomancy, or Virgilian lots

In early times, bibliomancy was one of the most easily accessible forms of divination. In its simplest form, it consisted of closing the eyes, opening a book, letting the finger move down a page, and then come to rest. The answer to a question lay in the word or phrase to which the finger pointed.

Both Jews and Christians used the Bible for divination purposes, partly because it was believed that divination was inspired by God, and partly because most households only owned a holy book. In other cultures, books of poetry were used, notably the works of Virgil (hence bibliomancy's alternative name, Virgilian lots). Bibliomancy was the preferred and constant link to divine wisdom on the part of kings, princes, and bishops from the fourth to fourteenth centuries AD.

Bibliomancy is still practiced by many religious groups today. More secular versions use any large tome—perhaps a thesaurus—and the methods can be changed according to taste. Selecting at random three numbers for a page, line, and word is another version of the system. In a library, a row of books can be chosen, then a number along a row to select the book, and so on. (The author selected a book, page, and word while writing this piece, resulting in the words "ancient art.")

Byblos

The word "bibliomancy" is derived from the Greek word *byblos*, meaning "paper." (The Phoenician city Byblos was once famous for the export of paper.)

Beatlemania

"We don't like their sound, and guitar music is on the way out."

Decca Recording Co., when rejecting the Beatles, 1962.

FAMOUS PREDICTIONS

Awesome prophecies have been made throughout history, some of which have come to pass. Old and new religions have predicted second comings and cataclysms. Today, as they are fed predictions of imminent disaster from psychics, astrologers, and religious fanatics, newspapers often note planetary alignments and total eclipses.

Desolation

There was a tendency for the ancients more often to predict future disaster than forthcoming periods of pleasure and joy.

The gloom of the ancients

"All terrestrial life and limb shall be consumed by fire during a planetary alignment in [AD July 2001]. The fire will be followed by a great flood in October, when the same planets are conjoined in the sign of Capricorn."

Berosus, the Chaldean astronomer, second century BC

"Another king shall arise out of Syria, born from an evil spirit, the overthrower and destroyer of the human race, who shall destroy that which is left by the former evil, together with himself... Power will be given him to desolate the whole earth for forty-two months."

Origen, who died in AD 254

"The church will be punished because the majority of her members, high and low, will become so perverted. The church will sink deeper and deeper until she will at last seem to be extinguished, and the succession of Peter and the other Apostles to have expired."

Nicholas of Flüh, fifteenth century

The atom bomb

The atom bomb has had many past predictions allocated to it, although of course the attributions were made after the event.

"Many and terrible signs will appear in the sky, the sun will darken and will show itself bloody-red. One will be able to see two moons at the same time for four hours long."
Caesarius of Heisterbach (1180–1240)

"The third millennium is the moment of the third great war. France is destroyed; the earth shakes . . ."
Liber Vaticinationem Quodam, AD 350

Recent Predictions

Jeane Dixon and Edward Cayce made startling predictions—some amazingly accurate, others hopelessly wrong.

Jeane Dixon predicted the assassinations of John and Robert Kennedy, and foresaw that Ronald Reagan would be president 18 years before he was sworn in. However she also predicted that the US would have its first woman president before 1990 and that in 1999, Russian missiles would "rain down a nuclear holocaust" on American "coastal cities in the east and west."

Edgar Cayce predicted World War I and World War II, the 1929 stock market crash, and the lifting of the Depression in 1933. He also claimed, however, that by 1998 California's coastline would be changed, Japan would disappear into the sea, and the Arctic and Antarctic regions would turn tropical.

Moon landing

Even psychics have their bad days—Jeane Dixon predicted that the Russians would be the first to land on the Moon.

Famous Psychics

Edgar Cayce
For most of his life, the psychic Edgar Cayce was able to give great insights into almost any question imaginable.

Mother Shipton, Jeane Dixon, and Edgar Cayce were all famous for making startlingly accurate predictions.

"Mother Shipton"

"Mother Shipton" was born in 1488 in Norfolk, England, and died in 1561. Many of her prophecies were realized during her own lifetime. Although her strange verses seem to have significant indications for our times, they are open to the widest of interpretations.

"A carriage without horse will go, disaster fill the world with woe.
In London, Primrose Hill shall be in center hold a bishop's see.
Around the world men's thoughts will fly, quick as the twinkling of an eye.
And water shall great wonders do, How strange, and yet it shall come true.
Through towering hills proud men shall ride, no horse or ass move by his side.
Beneath the water, men shall walk, shall ride, shall sleep, shall even talk.
And in the air men shall be seen, in white and black and even green.
A great man shall come and go, for prophecy declares it so."

Jeane Dixon

Jeane Dixon, a twentieth-century American prophet from Washington, DC, became renowned for her amazing accuracy. As early as 1952, she predicted the assassination of John F. Kennedy, when, in Washington's St. Matthew's Cathedral, she had a vision of the White House and a blue-eyed man standing at the door. At the same time, she heard a voice say that a Democrat who would become president in 1960 would be assassinated while in office. Early in 1963, she began to have new premonitions about this and made several attempts to warn President Kennedy of the danger she saw ahead. On Friday, November 22, she told friends: "This is the day it will happen." That afternoon, Kennedy was assassinated in Dallas, Texas.

Edgar Cayce

The American prophet Edgar Cayce gave evidence of his talents from an early age. While asleep, he would give people health advice and other information he claimed to know nothing about while awake. His responses have come to be called "readings." The records of his psychic readings today constitute one of the largest bodies of intuitive information to be produced by a single individual and cover dreams, meditation, reincarnation, and prophecy. They have provided the basis for over 300 books on his life.

NUMEROLOGY

The founder of the science of numbers is generally accepted to have been Pythagoras (about 580–500 BC). The belief that each number has a resonance and vibration that is unique to itself later developed further—into what we now call numerology. ⚘ Over the centuries, our fascination with numbers has resulted in the evolution of various systems for making judgements and prophecies based on this numerological system involving the nine numbers.

The Personal Numbers

The most popular system of numerology in the world today is based on our individual information at birth. This comprises our date of birth and our name.

The birth number

Your birth number indicates your vocational abilities. It reveals the natural powers and energies that you were born with and indicates how you will establish yourself and find your place in the world.

The system whereby you can discover your birth number is simple. Taking the date of birth of, say, June 14, 1968, we then translate it into complete numerical form by using the number of the month of June, which is 6 (June being the sixth month). Having thus arrived at the numbers 14, 6, and 1968, we then add all of these numbers together: 1+4+6+1+9+6+8 = 35. To produce a final single number, we now add 3+5 to produce 8, the birth number of a person born on June 14, 1968.

The destiny number

Your destiny number reveals your life's purpose, your opportunities, and how you can best act to achieve your greatest potential.

To find your destiny number, use the alphabet and your name. Consulting the table opposite, add together the numerical values of all of the letters in your full name at birth. Continue to add the resulting numbers together until you arrive at a single number.

For the name Mary Jeanette Smith, for example, we would find the destiny number by doing the following.

MARY = 4+1+9+7 = 21
JEANETTE = 1+5+1+5+5+2+2+5 = 26
SMITH = 1+4+9+2+8 = 24

By adding the numbers 21, 26, and 24 together, we come up with a total of 71. We now can now add the numbers 7 and 1 together to find that Mary Jeanette Smith's destiny number is the number 8.

The life-change number

For one reason or another, we may make, or have changes made to, the name that was given to us at birth. Although the destiny number remains the root indicator of our behavior and potential, we act out whatever destiny is ours in the manner signified by the life-change number.

To find your life-change number, use your changed name to work out a final number in the same manner as for your destiny number, described opposite.

Destiny and Life-Change Numbers Table

1	A	J	S
2	B	K	T
3	C	L	U
4	D	M	V
5	E	N	W
6	F	O	X
7	G	P	Y
8	H	Q	Z
9	I	R	

Using the example of Mary Jeanette Smith given opposite, if the name Mary is dropped, the life-change number would be worked out as follows.

JEANETTE = 1+5+1+5+5+2+2+5 = 26

SMITH = 1+4+9+2+8 = 24

By adding together the numbers 26 and 24 we arrive at a total of 50, which, added together, results in 5. The lady above would, therefore, have been destined to have been a number "8" person, but would have chosen to manifest those qualities in a "5" manner, because she chose to use the name Jeanette Smith rather than Mary Jeanette Smith.

Three

Pleasure-loving, self-expressive, creative, and always ready for fun. A number that keeps its natives young.

NUMBERS 1 TO 7

Numbers may be applied to all events in life. The manner in which they reflect people's aptitudes and character tendencies is an integral part of the cosmic plan. Those expert in numerology use numbers to determine the best time for major moves and activities. Numerology can be used to decide when to invest, marry, travel, change jobs, or move home. Being aware of the power of numbers gives one an insight into the possible outcome of events concerning their influence.

Positive: original, individual, creative, inventive, determined, courageous, and energetic.
Negative: aggressive, dominant, willful, impulsive, boastful, cynical, contrary, and egotistical.

Positive: diplomatic, a mediator, considerate, sensitive, tactful, and persuasive.
Negative: self-conscious, timid, shy, cunning, indecisive, insincere, and manipulative.

Positive: imaginative, inspirational, creative, self-expressive, optimistic, happy, and pleasure-loving.
Negative: extravagant, selfish, self-centered, overtalkative, having scattered energies, and overpossessive.

Positive: possesses application, concentration, practicality, a sense of values, seriousness, determination, and ambition.
Negative: stubborn, unimaginative, slow, exact, contrary, and having fixed opinions.

Positive: versatile, resourceful, progressive, energetic, curious, and possessing freedom of thought and new ideas.
Negative: restless, moody, impatient, hasty, discontented, and dissatisfied.

Positive: idealistic, artistic, humanitarian, unselfish, harmonious, and domesticated.
Negative: outspoken, dutiful, obstinate, slow in making decisions, self-sacrificing, and self-righteous.

Four
Practical, scientific, serious, with good application to painstaking tasks. A powerful number for achieving long-term ambitions.

Positive: specialist, technological, inventive, meditative, thoughtful, skillful, charming, and intelligent.
Negative: suspicious, repressive, unreasonable, overanalytical, argumentative, independent, and cynical.

Interpreting Numbers 1 to 7

The Sun
The center of our solar system represents the utmost creative drive and life force, as does the number 1.

Once you have discovered your personal numbers, consult the interpretations below for your own character outline.

1 The number 1 is ruled by the Sun and all that is strong, individual, and creative. It is the number of leaders, innovators, and winners, as well as of dictators. These people can often be ruthless, self-centered, and stubborn, and will probably be more enthusiastic about their chosen vocations and lifelong careers than their intimate relationships.

2 The number 2 is ruled by the Moon. Passive, gentle, and artistic, people ruled by 2 are more inclined to ideas than action. Extremely inventive, they can be less dynamic about making their ideas concrete. They usually have a great deal of charm and intuition, but may suffer from lack of confidence and also be changeable, oversensitive, and depressive.

3 Ruled by Jupiter, 3 people are talented, energetic, and self-disciplined, and usually succeed in their chosen occupations. Ambitious, conscientious, and independent, they love to be in control. Their outer persona may hide a deeper spirituality, since 3 is the number of the Trinity.

4 The number 4 is ruled by Uranus. These people are usually steady, practical, helpful, and have great endurance. Typically friendly, they rarely impose their natural sense of wrong or right on others and like the good things in life, including company.

5 Ruled by Mercury, 5 is the number of the intellect. These people are mercurial, alert, curious, impulsive, quick-thinking, sharp-tempered, and highly strung. They are good at making money and quickly recover from failure.

6 The number 6 is ruled by Venus. These people are concerned with the home, love, and family life and are reliable and trustworthy, but also obstinate. They need harmony and beauty and find it easier to make friends than people born under any of the other numbers. Despite a dislike of discord, they can be obstinate fighters.

7 The number 7 is ruled by Neptune. These people often have a restless love of travel and the sea. Rarely interested in everyday, material things, they often have an otherworldly, philosophical, or spiritual outlook. Often highly intuitive—even clairvoyant—they may exert a magnetic influence over others, but may also have a tendency to become too introverted.

Saturn
The ruler of the number 8 dominates the business and scientific worlds.

NUMBERS 8 AND 9

The final two numbers, 8 and 9, possess special qualities. Number 8 people are characterized by their drive and determination to succeed, so they are often successful in the field of business and commerce. Passionate and daring number 9 people are equally determined, though they are far more dramatic and bold in their approach and allow their hearts to rule their heads.

The young executive
Ambition and the drive to achieve some kind of prominence in business are easy for number 8 people. They have the necessary patience to wait for their opportunity.

Positive: *authoritative, powerful, efficient, organized, having executive ability, recognition, judgement, and strength.*
Negative: *overactive, tense, overambitious, repressive, demanding of recognition, forceful, and tense.*

Determination

The Martian quality of number 9 makes for boldness and daring, and an inability to give up, once set on a challenge.

Number 8

The number 8 is ruled by Saturn, and, although it can sometimes signify sorrow, this number is also associated with worldly success. These people have outstanding executive qualities, great willpower, and individuality, but may appear cold and matter-of-fact in their relationships. They do, however, have deep and intense feelings, and are often misunderstood by others, partly perhaps because they are so powerful.

Positive: *perfectionist, compassionate, idealistic, impressionable, forgiving, with a dramatic talent and love for art.*
Negative: *impulsive, changeable, moody, depressive, careless with finances, and a jack-of-all-trades.*

Number 9

The number 9 is ruled by Mars. It is sometimes considered the ultimate number, with special, or even sacred, significance, because, when it is multiplied by any other number, it continues to reproduce itself, for example, 3 x 9 = 27, 2 + 7 = 9). (Another strange characteristic of the number 9 is that, when it is added to a number according to the numerological system that we have been using, it does not change the value of that number; for instance, 8 + 9 = 17, 1+7 = 8.) These people are fighters; active, determined, and quarrelsome, they usually succeed after a struggle, but are also prone to accidents and injuries.

Other Techniques

Rose

Rose shares its harmonious number three with Valentine and Day, the perfect anniversary combination.

Once one has become familiar with the qualities of each number, it is simple to apply the principles of numerology to other areas of life. The names of the companies for which people work, for example, are sometimes compatible with their birth numbers (and sometimes not). House numbers, too, have different qualities: some denote quiet retreats, while others assure one of a noisy and sociable life. And, as the electronic age rushes in upon us, the concept of numerically positive websites and e-mail addresses may become an interesting new area for our experiments.

Although none of the numbers is unlucky, some will work better for you than others at different periods of your life. It is interesting to review your life, calculating the numbers of people whom you no longer see, or the places that you now rarely visit, but that have been important to you in the past. In this way you can begin to distil a pattern of numbers that will help you to achieve your operational and pleasurable best.

Gemetria and strange coincidences

The early Hebrew cabbalists used an entirely different numerical magical system, known as gemetria, for the Hebrew alphabet, and, according to this, the numerical equivalents of the various letters soar into the thousands. Documents were written in which the real meaning was not in the words, but in the symbols described by the numerical values. From this was derived the "number of the Beast," 666, which has featured prominently in so many horror movies.

Expanding on this theme, if we use our system for numbering ordinary words, we may often find strange coincidences, such as the following: heaven, hell, and man are all number "1s"; angel, peace, woman, tree, and rose are all number "3s"; and devil, hate, and sword are all number "7s."

The Kabbala

The Kabbala is the "tree of life" in Judaism. It is the foundation for an ancient mystical interpretation of the Bible that was first transmitted orally and reached the height of its influence in the late Middle Ages. It is significant in Hasidism, a mystical Jewish movement founded in Poland in the eighteenth century, which is still influential in Jewish life, particularly in Israel and New York.

The Kabbala is basically a method for understanding the psychology and behavior of human beings and a code of ethics whose purpose is to lead people to the ways of goodness and, ultimately, to God.

UNUSUAL
DIVINATION SYSTEMS

Our desire to use random, or chance, happenings to predict the future has led to almost anything being used for divination. Most of us have at some time carefully picked our way to school by avoiding stepping on cracks in the sidewalk, believing that if we succeeded the teacher might forget to ask for the homework that we hadn't done. Petals plucked from flowers have told us about love, while dandelions have told us the time. Our past ingenuity has known no bounds, and some of the stranger manifestations of this are documented on the following pages.

Strange Divination

The naming
Attraction to and dislike for certain names relates to our conditioning and experience of others with those names.

From the bizarre to the very gruesome, here are some of the more unusual methods that have been used for divinatory purposes.

Onomancy
Onomancy is a form of divination involving the meaning of a person's name. A child's name is believed to reflect and influence the kind of person that the child will become.

Maculomancy
Maculomancy interprets the shape, color, and placement of birthmarks or moles on the body. On the ear they denote great wealth; on the center of the forehead, enterprise.

Metopomancy
Metopomancy concerns reading the lines of the forehead. The forehead is divided into seven planetary areas, and the interpretations follow similar rules to those of palmistry.

Apantomancy
Apantomancy is a divination system based on chance encounters with animals. These generally predict good or bad fortune for a short period. To see a goat unexpectedly is said to be fortunate, and although a solitary lamb promises peace and happiness, a flock of sheep moving toward you is highly fortunate.

Belomancy and cleromancy
Belomancy is a form of divination using arrows, or any marked sticks, which are thrown into the air, their landing positions then being noted and

interpreted. This method is generally used for "Yes" or "No" questions, with crossed arrows giving a negative answer.

Cleromancy uses several-sided objects, such as sticks, bones, or shells, with symbols or marks on each side for prognostications. These are thrown onto a cloth decorated with figures, upon which they take on special significance.

Epatoscomancy

Epatoscomancy is divination through the examination of animal entrails. It was very popular in Rome, Greece, Japan, Sumeria, and other ancient civilizations and is still practiced in parts of Burma and Borneo.

Gelomancy

Gelomancy is divination from observing human sounds other than the spoken word, notably laughter. This form of fortune-telling once used the utterances and ravings of mentally disturbed or insane people.

Cats

These creatures have featured strongly in all forms of magic and divination since their veneration by the ancient Egyptians. Even now we attribute a sixth sense, nine lives, and lucky or unlucky omens to them.

USING THE ENVIRONMENT

Animals, fire, clouds, color—the world that surrounds us has provided tools for divination for centuries. Some of the following systems of divination—most of which have been employed since ancient times—may be familiar to you.

Felidomancy

This is based on the movements and behavior of cats. The ancient Egyptian cat goddesses Pasht and Sekhmet raised the feline to the rank of deity, and the cat's association with witches may be connected with this sacred past. Some vestiges of felidomancy may be seen in folk sayings like: a cat's sneeze denotes rain; a cat at a wedding ensures a happy and long relationship.

Colorology

Colorology is divination using the brilliance of auras, the halos of transparent color surrounding our bodies. Blues are said to glow around people who feel for others; reds around the adventurous. A yellow aura indicates strong imaginative qualities; green, a sociable being; brown, dependability; black, rebellion; and violet, creativity.

Lampadomancy

Divination using a candle flame is called lampadomancy. A large, bright flame denotes exceptionally good fortune, for instance, and a legacy of lampadomancy can be seen in the practice of blowing out all of the candles on a birthday cake to make a wish come true.

Aeromancy

Aeromancy involves the interpretation of cloud formations. We retain vestiges of the method in our continued use of such sayings as a "mackerel sky, twelve hours dry," "red sky at night, shepherd's delight; red sky in the morning, shepherd's warning," and so on.

Spodomancy

Spodomancy is divination by fire. A paper is inscribed with a message or question and is then set alight. The reading is done according to the behavior, color, and twists and turns of the smoke and flames. In ancient times, the shape that the ashes made was also read, much in the same way as tea leaves are read.

Alectryomancy

Divination based on the behavior of animals is known as alectryomancy. Once, the most popular method was to introduce a cock or hen into a circle marked with the letters of the alphabet, in front of each of which was placed a grain of wheat. The significance of the order in which the fowl would peck at the grains was noted and interpreted. A present-day version of this system is popular in many places, particularly Singapore. A question is asked, and a trained bird will then select an answer written on one of a series of papers held in a rack.

FURTHER READING

The author's websites are as follows:
www.eltarot.co.uk
www.littlestars.com
www.moonoracle.com

Astrology

A. T. MANN, *Time Life Astrology*, Element Books, 1991

JULIA AND DEREK PARKER, *Parker's Astrology*, Dorling Kindersley, 1994

JULIA AND DEREK PARKER, *Sun & Moon Signs*, Dorling Kindersley, 2000

JULIA AND DEREK PARKER, *Parker's Prediction Pack*, Dorling Kindersley, 1999

JULIA AND DEREK PARKER, *Parker's Astrology Pack*, Dorling Kindersley, 1997

JULIA AND DEREK PARKER, *KISS Astrology*, Dorling Kindersley, 2000

Astrological software for calculating charts and even printing complete interpretations is available, ranging from nothing to $300 to $400 in the US. There are also excellent shareware programs that can be tried first and paid for later.

www.astrologer.com
Good astrological links.

www.starscreen.co.uk
A daily horoscope screensaver based on transits to the birthchart.

www.world-of-wisdom.com
Good, clear, shareware software that is easy to work with.

Chinese astrology

THEODORA LAU, *The Handbook of Chinese Horoscopes*, Harper & Row, 2000

Divination

C. EASSON, *The Complete Guide to Divination*, Piatkus, 1998

www.knopfler.com/divination
General divination material on just about everything.

Dowsing

TOM GRAVES, *Diviner's Handbook: A Guide to the Timeless Art of Dowsing*, Inner Traditions, 1990

Geomancy

N. PENNICK, *The Oracle of Geomancy*, Princeton Holmes Publishing Group, 1998

STEPHEN SKINNER, *Terrestrial Astrology, Divination by Geomancy*, Routledge & Kegan Paul, 1980

I Ching

ALFRED DOUGLAS, *The Oracle of Change*, Victor Gollancz Ltd., 1971

S. KARCHER, *How to Use the I Ching: A Guide to Working with the Oracle of Change*, Element Books, 1998

RICHARD WILHELM (trs.) AND C. F. BAYNES, *The I Ching Book of Changes*, Princeton University Press, 1967

Numerology

Ancient Wisdom for the New Age: Numerology, New Holland, 1998

KRISTYNA ARCATI, *Numerology*, Headway 1999

SONIA DUCIE, *The Complete Illustrated Guide to Numerology*, Element Books, 1999

Palmistry

CHEIRO, *Cheiro's Language of the Hand*, Random House, 1999

CHEIRO, *Cheiro's Palmistry for All*, Corgi Books, 1975

Runes

RALPH BLUM, *The Book of Runes*, Michael Joseph, 1993

D. JASON COOPER, *Using the Runes*, Aquarian Press, 1986

Scrying

ANDREW HARMAN, *The Scrying Game*, Orbit, 1996

DONALD TYSON, *Scrying for Beginners*, Llewellyn Publications, 1997

Tarot

BILL BUTLER, *The Definitive Tarot*, Rider and Company, 1975

K. MCCORMACK, *The Definitive Book of Tarot*, David Westnedge, 1989

There is a great deal of material devoted to the tarot on the Internet, and some of the best sites are given below.

www.artoftarot.com
Michele's Tarot Page is about the best and most informative tarot site to be found on the web. It contains reviews of many tarot decks.

www.eltarot
The Elemental Tarot has excellent tarot software.

www.kenaz.com
A good site for tarot, astrology, and other divination methods.

www.wicce.com
Wicce's Tarot Collection gives plenty of information and reviews.

INDEX

ACKNOWLEDGMENTS

Thanks to Caroline Earle, whose editing kept me down to earth when my altered states became just a little too distant. Thanks to Caroline Smith my wife, tarot inspiration, and information source. Thanks finally to my collection of old almanacs, books, tarot cards, teacups, and pendula, and a lifetime's alternative clutter.

The publisher would like to thank Sara Collins, Clarinda Hall, Abdoulie Marong, Jo Maxwell-Gumbleton, Kay Macmullan, and Farhana Rahman for help with photography.

PICTURE ACKNOWLEDGMENTS

Every effort has been made to trace copyright holders and obtain permission. The publishers apologize for any omissions and would be pleased to make any necessary changes at subsequent printings.

Tarot Cards

The illustrations on the following pages are reproduced by permission of AGM AGMüller, CH-8212 Neuhausen/Switzerland www.tarotworld.com. Further reproduction prohibited. ©1982 AGM AGMüller, Switzerland. OTO Ordo Templi Orientis IHQ, 14180 Berlin. Aleister Crowley Thoth Tarot 22BL, 23BR.

Photographic Credits

Corbis:40 (Bettmann), 46TL (Christies), 86 (Reuters/Newmedia Inc.), 194 (Roger Wood), 198B (Scott T.Smith).
The Image Bank:130T, 130B.
Images Colour Library: 59, 102, 134T, 134/135, 218B.
NASA: 50/51 ALL, 199, 210T.
Stone/Getty One: 22BR, 48, 78B, 106, 110, 127, 138B, 179, 206, 207, 218T.
The Stock Market, London:158, 219T, 219B.
Superstock, London: 211.